Christopher Wood

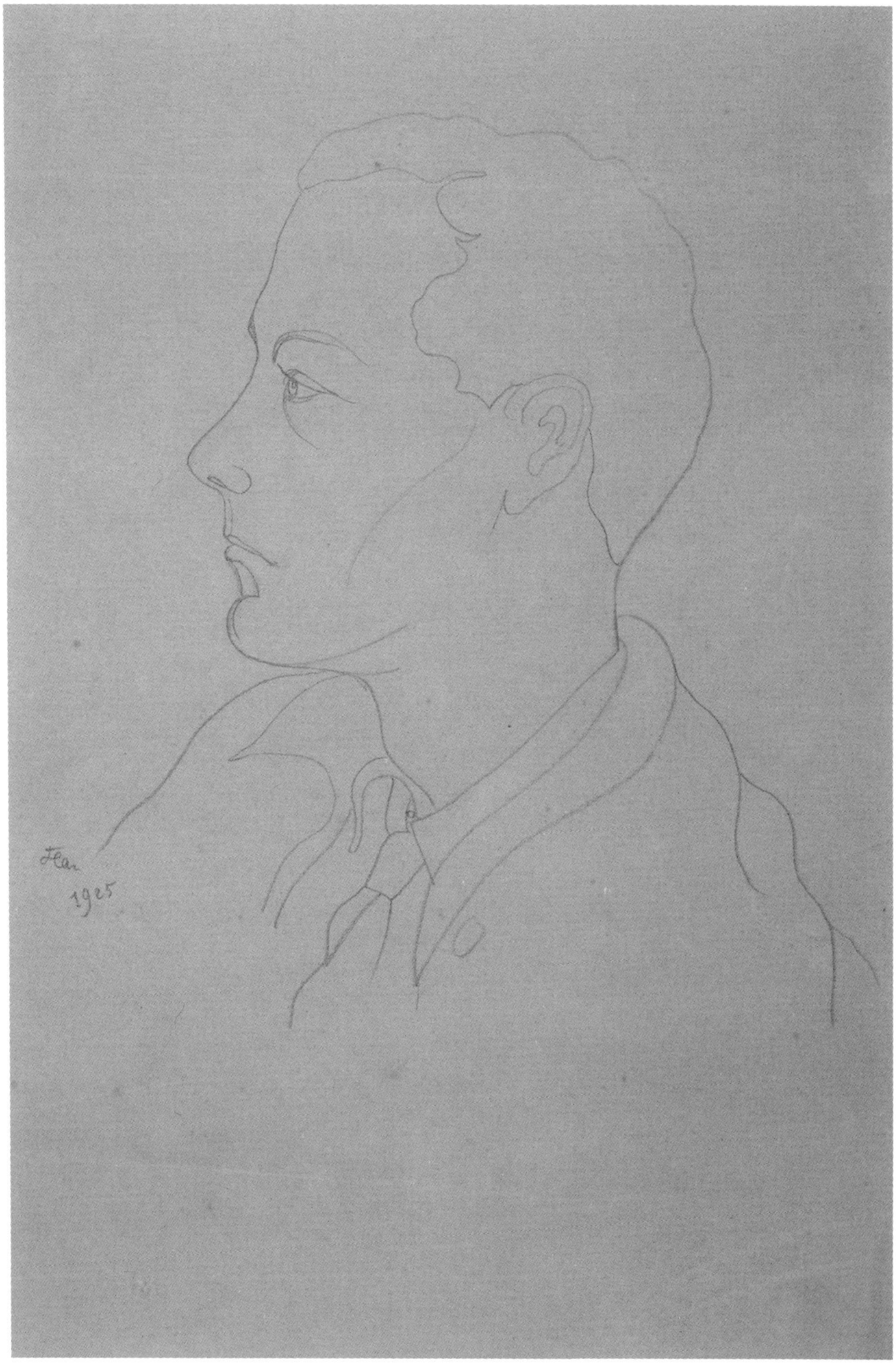
Jean
1925

André Cariou and Michael Tooby

Christopher Wood

A PAINTER BETWEEN TWO CORNWALLS

With essays by Françoise Steel-Coquet

Tate Gallery Publishing

Supported by Brittany Ferries
and The Yves Hervouet Research
Fund at Lancaster University for
Anglo-French Relations

This catalogue is published to accompany
the exhibition jointly organised by Tate Gallery
St Ives and the Musée des Beaux-Arts, Quimper

Tate Gallery St Ives
16 November 1996 – 20 April 1997

Musée des Beaux-Arts, Quimper
14 May – 31 August 1997

frontispiece
Jean Cocteau, *Portrait of Christopher Wood*, 1925,
pencil
The Dartington Hall Trust

front cover
Tréboul, 1930 (no.18), detail

back cover
The Fisherman's Farewell, 1928 (no.6)

ISBN 1 85437 224 6

A catalogue record for this publication
is available from the British Library

Published by order of the Trustees
of the Tate Gallery 1996
by Tate Gallery Publishing Limited,
Millbank, London SW1P 4RG

Translations by Michael Bird and
Miriam Darlington
Designed by Caroline Johnston
Printed in Great Britain by Balding + Mansell,
Kettering, Northamptonshire

Also available in French

Contents

Foreword

Painters have always loved both Cornwalls, Breton and English. In each place they have found not only sources of inspiration, in the landscape and the lively fishing harbours especially, but also a congenial atmosphere. A century ago, John Milner Kite stayed both at Newlyn and at Concarneau; around the same time, a number of other British landscape painters, including Robert Weir Allan and Terrick Williams, were attracted to Douarnenez and Tréboul. A little later Cedric Morris discovered, after St Ives, the shores of Douarnenez bay.

Christopher Wood first visited St Ives in 1926. Fascinated by the landscape, and later stimulated by his relationship with Ben and Winifred Nicholson and his meeting with Alfred Wallis, he found there an appropriate atmosphere for his work. Three years later, thanks to Pierre Colle and Max Jacob, Wood discovered Cornouaille, the Breton Cornwall. There he painted the fishing boats in the harbour and the life of the quays and small streets, just as he had done in England. In a body of work sadly cut short, the paintings he produced in the two Cornwalls comprise the apex of his creative work.

Tate Gallery St Ives opened in 1993, with the purpose of exhibiting the work of artists connected with the Cornish town. In the same year, the Musée des Beaux-Arts in Quimper, twelve miles from Douarnenez and Tréboul, reopened. The museum had been renovated and extended, and for the first time there was space for the installation of a room dedicated to Max Jacob and his friends. This new display included the only work by Christopher Wood that is still in France, his celebrated portrait of Jacob (no.13). It soon became apparent that the two institutions could join together to organise an exhibition that would present Christopher Wood's work in the two Cornwalls.

Our sincere thanks go to all the lenders, without whom the exhibition would not have been possible. We are also grateful to the Yves Hervouet Research Fund for their support of this publication, and to Brittany Ferries for their sponsorship-in-kind for research travel and shipping between the two venues. Our gratitude also goes to Françoise Steel-Coquet, not only for her contribution to the catalogue but for other assistance with the exhibition. At Tate Gallery St Ives, Matthew Rowe is to be thanked not only for his catalogue entries but also for his help in researching and coordinating the project. We are grateful to Richard Ingleby for the variety of ways in which he has assisted the exhibition and publication.

André Cariou
Director, Musée des Beaux-Arts, Quimper

Nicholas Serota
Director, Tate Gallery

Michael Tooby
Curator, Tate Gallery St Ives

Christopher Wood: On the Edge of the World

Michael Tooby

I seem to live on the edge of the world. But what a world it is, I love this place and could stay here for ever if I had those around me for whom I care. Each day there is a new thrill here, wonderful sunshine terrific storms – each thing is at its best for this place is a picture gallery of only the good pictures and one feels its good quality so much that one hardly wants to seek another. Still its [sic] time to do so. I expect I shall soon be back again but it will be hard to leave it. You seem to feel this place as I do, I feel it belongs in a sense to me although less + less do I wish to possess things in a voluminous sense …

Letter to Winifred Nicholson from Christopher Wood
St Ives, December 1928 (TGA 8618)

The place is very like St Ives. In fact everything here looks like Cornwall which makes me want to be back there with you. If only I could have last summer just as it was I would be very glad. It always takes a week or two to know what one wants to do, and until then one sometimes has bad moments of wondering whether one will ever be able to work again.

Postcard to Ben Nicholson from Christopher Wood
Douarnenez, July 1929 (TGA 8618)

I wish very much you were all here it is such a beautiful place + so full of interest + very quiet + very good food in this clean hotel. The only other occupant here is Max Jacob the poet who came to join me + we meet only at meals and work all day which is an amusing and excellent arrangement.

I feel my work going ahead getting stronger and a little more serious in design and more direct in idea and less naive. I have painted a good deal; of architecture and less boats for a change + this seems to make it easier to make a quieter composition. I am very amused by everything I see + I find the postcards of this country very helpful … The bay of Douarnenez is looking beautiful, very blue. There have been a lot of fêtes here lately and all the white houses have little bouquets of bright flowers pinned to them + the narrow streets are strewn with flowers and palm leaves put in the shape of the sun. All the larger fishing boats are in the harbour being repainted for the … fishing season, the sailors are very gay full of songs and drinks. I will leave just as the summer visitors arrive so I won't have the pleasure of seeing the beautiful white beaches covered in ugly people and banana skins'

Letter to Winifred and Ben Nicholson from Christopher Wood
Hôtel Ty-Mad, Tréboul, July 1930 (TGA 8618)

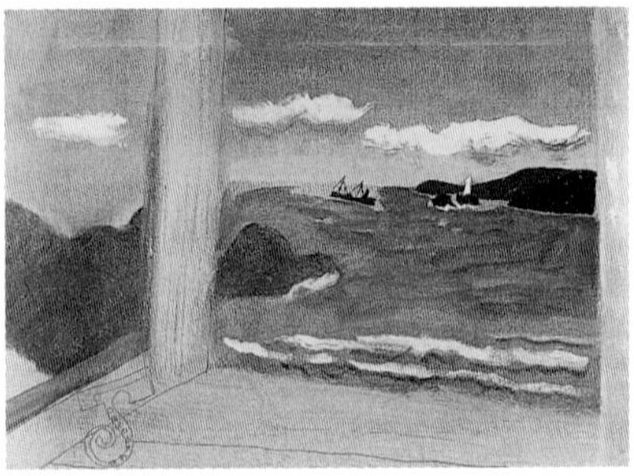

fig.1 Ben Nicholson, *1931 (St Ives Bay, sea with boats)*, 1928–31, oil. Manchester City Art Galleries

In December 1928 Christopher Wood left St Ives, at the end of his second stay there. His first stay had been for a little over two months in the early autumn of 1926. This time he had been in the town since mid September, following the now famous visit with Ben Nicholson one day in August, when they had first met Alfred Wallis. Just over seven months later, having spent the winter and spring in London, Paris and touring in northern France, Wood arrived in Douarnenez, in the Cornouaille region, in late July 1929.

Wood remained in and around Douarnenez until mid September. He then followed his lover Froska Munster to Paris, afterwards travelling to London, and returned to west Cornwall to visit Mousehole in the spring of 1930. After attending the opening in June of his exhibition at the Galerie Georges Bernheim, he went again to Cornouaille, staying in the town of Tréboul for most of June and July. He returned to England to meet his mother, and was killed by a train at Salisbury station on 21 August 1930. He was twenty-nine years old.

Douarnenez is a harbour town, twenty kilometres from Quimper, the capital of Cornouaille, a district within Finistère, Brittany. Tréboul, immediately adjacent, has beaches and a number of hotels. The excerpts from his correspondence to Ben and Winifred Nicholson quoted above eloquently describe Wood's feelings of revelation in discovering the affinities between Cornouaille and the west of Cornwall.

Differences between the two places are now as evident as similarities, as anyone who visits them both will discover. In Wood's day, the typical travellers coming and going in Cornwall and Cornouaille were the mariners of the fishing fleet, even then in decline from its heyday in the late nineteenth century. Today, the visitor from Cornwall who travels to Cornouaille via northern Brittany may be particularly struck by the busy dual-carriageways filled with trucks. The traffic is an indication of the number of industrial and business complexes that exist in a growing concentration of urban developments – a sharp contrast to the largely derelict industrial landscape of Cornwall, where there has been little redevelopment.

For the visitor arriving in Quimper, the cathedral and square, museums, shops, cafés, small businesses and co-ordinated public transport contribute to an atmosphere which, while being no less locally self-aware and historically defined than the large towns of Cornwall, seems much more shaped by modern Europe. The city is also concerned to express its local history in a contemporary manner. It recently dedicated a new bridge over its river as a memorial to the poet Max Jacob, who was arrested as a Jew by the Nazis during the occupation of France, and died in Drancy concentration camp in 1944.

As the visitor travels on towards Douarnenez and Tréboul, however, images that recall Cornwall become more evident. Most immediate is the topography of dark rocks, green outcrops and sandy beaches. Small cottages and town houses predominate over post-war housing and industrial development.

In these rural areas it is even still possible occasionally to see an older woman wearing traditional black dress and white lace cap. However, in Douarnenez itself is perhaps the most telling aspect of local modernisation: the old harbour, where Christopher Wood walked and drew, is now a museum. Where Wood watched the timber hulls being built or repaired, tourists can do

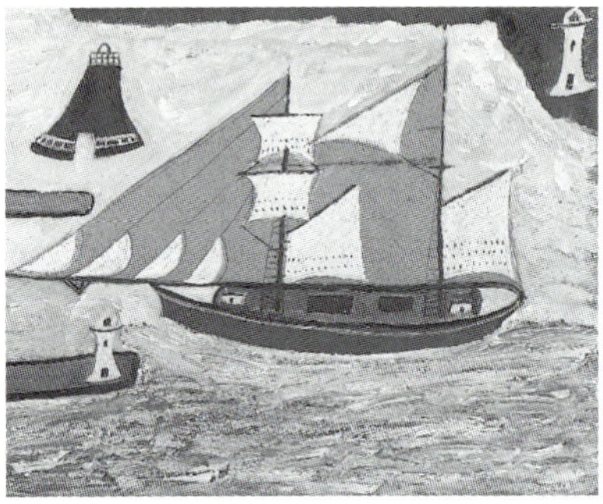

fig.2 Alfred Wallis, *The Blue Ship*, ?c.1934, oil. Tate Gallery

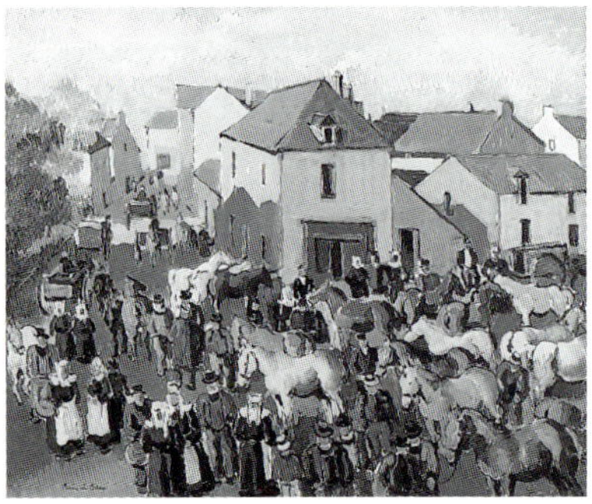

fig.3 Pierre de Belay, *The Horse Martket at Rosporden*, 1928. Musée des Beaux-Arts, Quimper

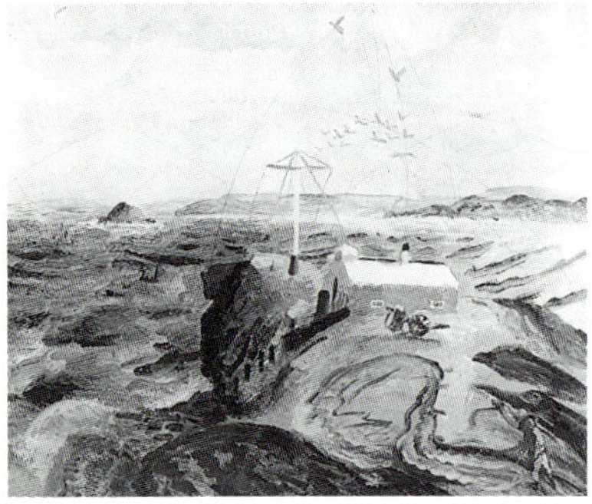

fig.4 Winifred Nicholson, *Pilchard Nets, The Island, St Ives*, 1928, oil. The Dartington Hall Trust

the same – but as part of an educational workshop held alongside sheds with exhibits illustrating the history of boat building and the maritime industry.

Similarities between Cornwall and Cornouaille are evident in much of the art history of the two regions. By the 1920s, both had seen half a century of academic and plein-air painters produce large-scale epic narratives and small-scale genre scenes. In both regions these were mainly made by artists whose careers were bound up with the institutions of their respective capitals. While the Breton 'colony' was centred on Concarneau and the Cornish on Newlyn, the leading artists in both centres continued to regard their principal exhibiting base as the annual exhibitions of the academies in Paris or London. Many maintained studios in the capitals while building their careers around depicting the regions with which they were associated in the public's mind.

However, both Concarneau and Newlyn were eventually affected by encounters with modernism in nearby towns. In Brittany, Gauguin was the best-known figure in the school of Pont Aven, while much later, Wood was to be a primary influence in the emergence of St Ives as a centre of debate around a local school of modernist artists.

In St Ives, Wood showed no interest in the academic tradition. His letters from there make no mention of the professional artists occupying the Porthmeor Studios. Instead, the letters from the extended visit of 1928 are full of references to Alfred Wallis, the old sailor and junk-merchant who had recently taken up painting, in a style that was child-like (fig.2). Wood was staying in a house at the end of Back Road West, on Porthmeor Beach. While he obviously delighted in being a few doors along from Wallis, it is apparent that he did not register that just several doors further were some of the best-known artists of the day, who in 1926 had opened one of the Porthmeor Studios as an exhibition space for the St Ives Society of Artists – a group which was likewise ignored by Wood.

In Brittany, Wood spent his first visit with the artist Pierre Colle and his second in the company of Max Jacob (fig.5), again eschewing the most obvious artistic communities of the area. Through Jacob he may have met other artists such as Pierre de Belay (fig.3), but they were all probably drawn together much more by common interests in depicting and discussing vernacular customs and the local surroundings than by explicitly shared artistic programmes.

While in Douarnenez and Tréboul in 1929 and again in 1930, it seems Wood attempted to maintain a simple routine. In seeing the echoes and resonances between Cornouaille and Cornwall, he sought the balance and focus in his working life he had first discovered with Ben and Winifred Nicholson in 1928 in Cumberland and St Ives. The imagery in his work shows how his surroundings also prompted a private symbolism of rootedness, countered by a sense of imminent change and decay.

In St Ives, Wallis had appeared to Wood as an example of honesty and sincerity in his approach to work. In parallel, the participants in the fêtes and religious ceremonies of Tréboul and Douarnenez gave him an impression of maintaining their own honest traditions of devotion and celebration. The image of the fishing boat was a literal connection between the two Cornwalls. The boatbuilders and sailors of Douarnenez, immersed in the traditions of their trade, represented to Wood a depth of intent to which he could only aspire.

The fishing boat, whilst implying continuity, also suggested the dangerous

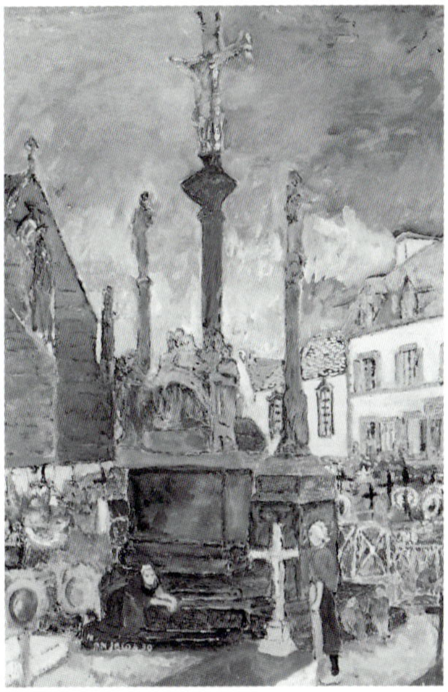

fig.5 Max Jacob, *The Calvary at Guengat*, 1930, gouache. Musée des Beaux-Arts, Quimper

journey on open seas. The skeletal form of the boat under repair or construction became nothing more than the carcass, washed up on the land. The Calvary, the crucifix characteristically seen in squares and on promontories, represented the presence of death and redemption in everyday life. More than in Cornwall, Wood's paintings in Breton are interspersed with private images. These suggest moments of calm: they are epiphanies of a private calm – a figure in a hotel room (no.31), a figure sleeping on a beach (no.26) – or of private devotion revealed to a stranger – a woman at prayer (no.20). These images provide an insight into the world to which Wood aspired to belong, in which there exists a communal identity and sense of security.

The narrative of Wood's career as presented in the present exhibition prompts consideration of the contexts of the two galleries at which it will be shown. In St Ives, Wood's work relates to the modernist tradition which forms the basis of the displays at Tate Gallery St Ives. Wood exists in St Ives as a moment in a story when he and Ben Nicholson, calling in from the wider world, chose to alert that world to one old man with an extraordinary obsession for painting. He was one of the artists who also brought about a change in the way in which the dramatic setting of the town was depicted.

In Quimper, Wood was again an intrigued visitor calling in from the wider world. It was here that he gradually began make use of images from postcards, translating the documentation of local topography and history into another form. His vision was at once fresh and informed by a search for essential truths behind the images of daily life and the reproduction of special events in tourist ephemera. Today, the art that Wood and others made still acts as a transformation of a world more often represented as an image on a postcard or in a tourist brochure.

Christopher Wood and France

Françoise Steel-Coquet

Figures 7–15, 17, 19, 21 are taken from a photograph album owned by the Redfern Gallery, London, compiled in 1938 alongside Eric Newton's book (see p.27). Courtesy Tate Gallery Archive Photographic Collection

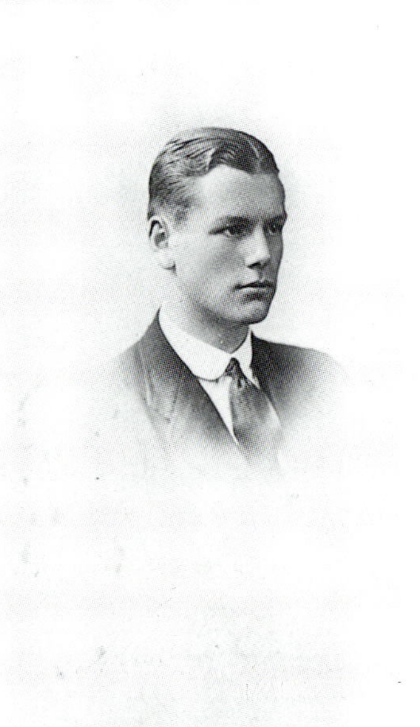

fig.6 Christopher Wood c.1920 (TGA 723)

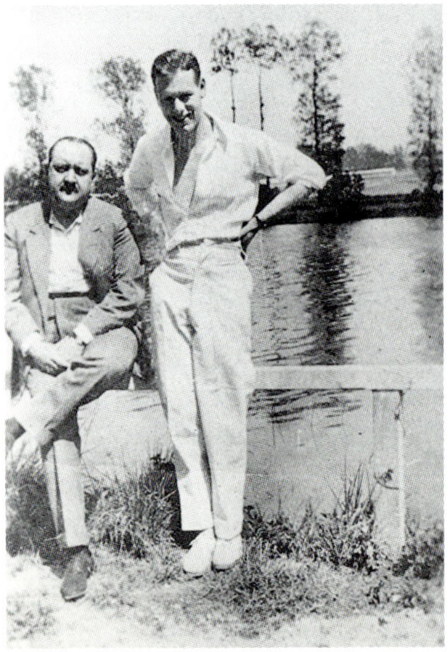

fig.7 Christopher Wood and Alphonse Kahn c.1924

Christopher Wood's life and work are dominated by ambiguities and contradictions. To all his French friends he appeared, both in himself and in his art, supremely British. Yet from the age of twenty, with the exception of a few visits to Cornwall and the north of England, and some brief forays to London, he spent almost the whole of his artistic career in France. It was there that he received his training as a painter, visiting the studios of the foremost contemporary artists (including Picasso's), assimilating their advice, and spending time in the Parisian art schools. His most frequent subjects are the landscapes and street scenes he painted of Paris, the Côte d'Azur and, above all, Brittany. From his earliest works, he was hailed as an artist of great talent by leading members of the Parisian intelligentsia, including Jean Cocteau, Max Jacob, René Crevel and Christian Bérard. After his death at the age of twenty-nine, however, a complete reversal of his fortunes took place. In England, a whole legend grew up around his personality and painting, together with a debate – periodically reactivated – concerning his place in British art. In France, on the other hand, apart from scattered references to him in memoirs of the 1920s, Christopher Wood was almost completely forgotten: this is the catalogue to the first exhibition of Wood's work to be shown in France since that put on by the Galerie Georges Bernheim in 1930.

Among the innumerable foreign artists who converged on Paris in the 1920s, none had a more auspicious beginning than Christopher Wood. It was at the instigation of the patron and collector Alphonse Kahn that he arrived in the French capital in March 1921, at the age of twenty. He was probably introduced to the wealthy banker by a mutual friend, Robert Tritton, a dealer specialising in precious Oriental artefacts. Giving up his office job in London, and with no artistic baggage other than the vague project of doing some painting, a basic knowledge of architecture left over from his short-lived studies, and a smattering of French, Wood did not think twice about accepting Kahn's invitation. Kahn has been described by Maurice Sachs in *La Décade de l'illusion* as:

> a great connoisseur of painting, whose word carried considerable influence in Paris. He had a taste for high quality carried to an extreme, and his exquisitely chosen, rare collection was equal in importance to the foremost American collections, gathering together magnificent paintings which altogether constitute one of France's treasures.[1]

Wood moved in to the banker's home, 41 avenue du Bois de Boulogne, and found himself plunged overnight into Parisian high society, a milieu from which he hardly ever parted company before the two last years of his life. On the walls of his mentor's apartment he found the works of such artists as Rembrandt, Turner and Fragonard alongside contemporary paintings by Matisse and Picasso. Kahn was a collector with a sharp eye and eclectic tastes, and his possessions also included Egyptian antiquities and medieval treasures. He undertook the young Englishman's artistic education, acting as his guide in museums, and taking him to the leading dealers in contemporary painting and the studios of artists. In an early letter to his mother, Wood described his new life: 'I have been in such a whirl of pictures, galleries, studios etc'.[2] And thanks to Kahn, he was soon able to see in perspective the two intertwined aspects of art: creation and patronage. For the rest of his life, he was to be torn between these two poles – the visceral desire to paint, and the necessity of pleasing those patrons with buying power whose whims determined the barometer of the art market. For the time being, instead of experiencing the harsh realities of bohemian life, he lived at the centre of the most sophisticated artistic circles in the world, without even having served his apprenticeship as a painter. His lack of culture and his naivety left him open to all kinds of influences, and, if his nature remained neither critical nor judgmental, he nevertheless learned his lessons well and avidly.

It is undeniable that his good looks, noted by all those who knew him, facilitated his entry into Paris-centred circles. The Swiss writer Charles Albert Cingria said of him that he was: 'neither a soul nor a body; rather, it was like a light, a fine transparent glow of alabaster – one was taken aback by his presence as by a privilege.'[3] Other equally rapturous eulogies could be cited. Moreover, his youth, his good manners and his elegance, in which he seemed closer to his patrons than to his fellow painters, were accompanied by an accommodating sexuality which further endeared him in a milieu where bisexuality was rather the norm than the exception. Parisian high society had an appetite for the new; having miraculously survived the First World War, it was now solely concerned with having a good time and enjoying the arts. As the American journalist Janet Flanner wrote, every Parisian premiere 'caused conversation, criticism, animation, appreciation, pejoration, and when all the talk and the ink died down, they [were] found to have marked fragile but definite dates in the literate Parisian's mind.'[4] If high society occasionally rubbed shoulders with unshaven bohemia at such places as the café-cabaret Le Boeuf sur le Toit or the annual Bal des Quat'zarts of the Ecole des Beaux-Arts, it also knew how to keep its distance, in reality only opening its doors to established artists, such as Picasso, Cocteau and Bérard – the very artists Wood took as his models.

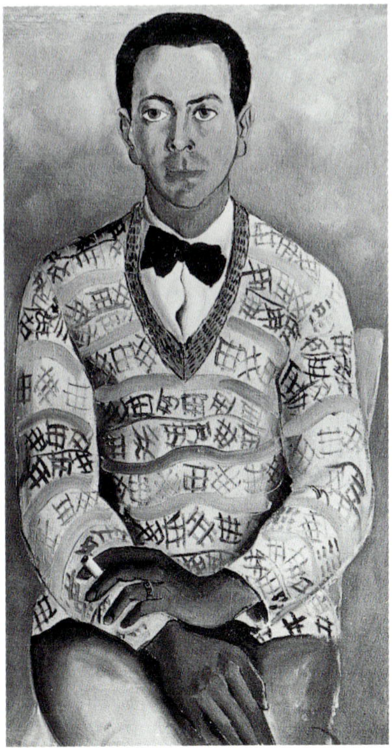

fig.8 *Portrait of J.A. Gandrillas*, 1926, oil. King George VI Art Gallery, Port Elizabeth, South Africa (EN 178)

A few weeks after his arrival in Paris, the young Englishman was introduced to an honorary Chilean diplomat, Antonio de Gandarillas (fig.8). Fourteen years older than Wood, Gandarillas was married but soon separated from his wife, Doña Maria. He was a man of great refinement and culture, well known in both Paris and London for his extravagant receptions, and he lived at the centre of an extensive circle of international contacts. His lavish life-style was partly financed by his gambling activities. In late 1921, Gandarillas financed Wood's own flat; in 1922 Wood effectively moved in to Gandarillas's vast apartment at 60 avenue Montaigne, where for the next six years the Chilean was to look after his material needs. In 1926, he fitted out for Wood an apartment-studio at 6 rue des Marronniers in fashionable Passy, where he had acquired three floors of an apartment block with terrace gardens. A deep and sincere friendship, together with a lasting gratitude, bound Wood to Gandarillas. These feelings were probably more important than the homosexual relationship that must also have brought them together.

Gandarillas's way of life, with its receptions, balls, and dinners, was almost wholly nocturnal. This allowed Wood to study during the daytime. Shortly

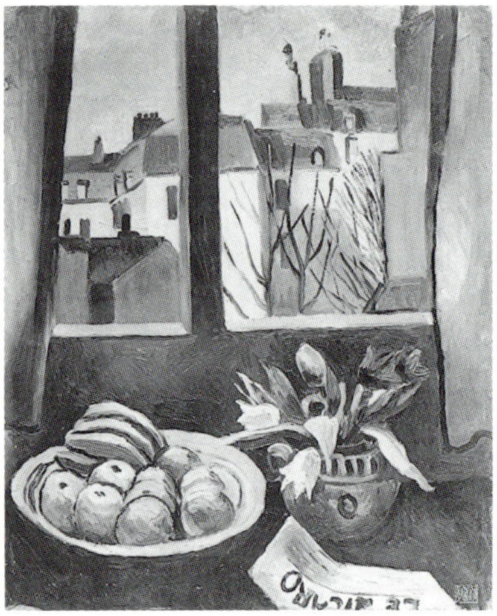

fig.9 *Studio Window, Rue des St. Peres*, 1923, oil. Private Collection (EN 20)

after he arrived in Paris he had rented a studio, first in rue de la Motte-Picquet then at 54 rue des Saints Pères (fig.9) (closer, interestingly, to the fashionable Faubourg St Germain than to the artists' quarter of Montmartre). He enrolled at the Académie Julian and the Grande Chaumière atelier, then at the Académie Montparnasse, where he was taught by André Lhote. He was later to study, if only briefly, with Maurice Denis. Aware of vast gaps in his cultural education, compared with those around him, Wood set about filling these in – as far as Gandarillas's frenetic life-style and his own far from robust constitution would allow.

The location of the diplomat's two apartments at Passy was to determine the aspect of Paris that Wood represented in his earliest works (figs.10, 11). For the rest of his life, he hardly looked beyond the Paris of the wealthy 'Beaux Quartiers', where, strangely coming full-circle, he was later to paint his two last canvases. There is an almost rural quality to his quickly sketched scenes: Passy and Neuilly are urban villages at the edges of which still lingers the Paris of Seurat and the Douanier Rousseau. Highly receptive to the poetry of place, Wood wrote to his mother: 'Paris is lovely … it is a ville magique and I love, love it and feel at home in it.' And on the same note:

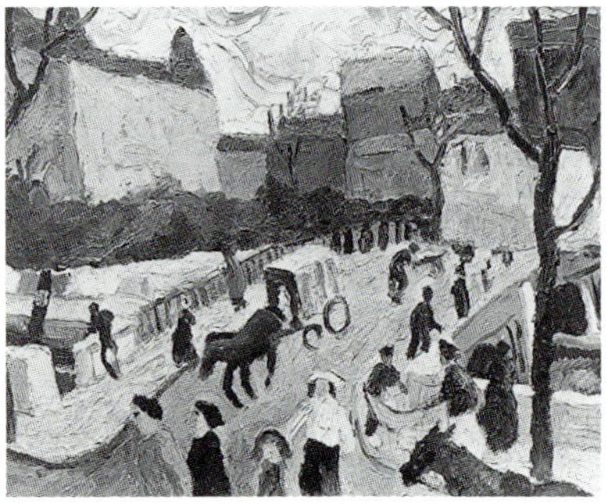

fig.10 *The Seine at Passy*, 1924, oil. Private Collection (EN 60)

> We went through the Bois [de Boulogne] with its lovely green velvetness – you could see right in – in the dark with the trees, the faint gleam of girls' frocks and bare arms, the black of the men's clothes, the lovely motor-cars with the beautiful South Americans with their dark skins and gleaming eyes clustered like bunches of flowers in the Hispano Suizas. Then out we went through the Porte de St Cloud and the crowd of gay laughing people who one sees so close from a motor car right into their faces. They are gay and wonderful along the Avenue de Neuilly where they are getting up the tall white poles with their coloured lights and funny coloured designs hanging from the sides, with their green trees and the white and green houses.[5]

Wood made drawings of men leaning on the zinc counters of cafés, families wandering amid joyless fairground shows, cyclists setting off for an outing; his scenes of Parisian streets and squares are handled in the manner of Utrillo.

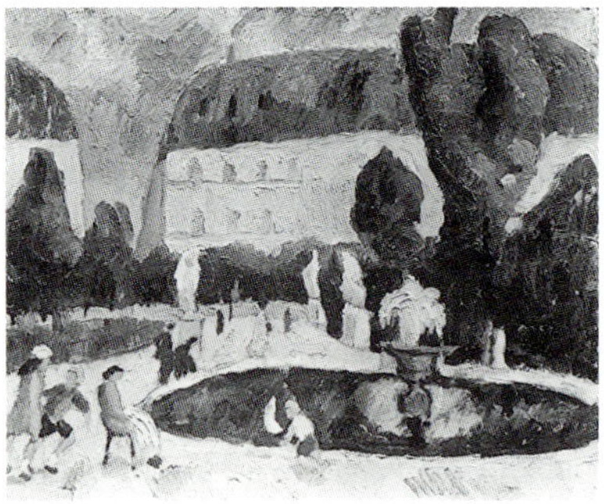

fig.11 *Gardens, St. Cloud*, 1924, oil. Private Collection (EN 32)

After a year spent almost entirely in travelling, to Turkey, North Africa and Sicily, on diplomatic visits to palaces around the world – endless upheavals that left him with little time in which to paint – Wood experienced a period of profound dissatisfaction. As his sense of vocation as a painter became progressively stronger, he felt himself torn between the glittering social life he was leading in Gandarillas's wake and the demands of his *métier*, prey to the insoluble dilemma that was to poison his life. To his mother he wrote of his feelings of terrible isolation, without anyone with whom he could discuss his work. Wood had neither the facility nor the inclination to adopt the role his brilliant friends were preparing for him, that of a fashionable society painter, following the example of the designer Adrian Drian, whom he at one time admired and dreamt of rivalling, but quickly rejected as a model. Gradually, he was to try to disavow the image of himself that he saw in others' eyes. He had already given up working for the couturier Edward Molyneux, for whom he had designed posters and fans. To his mother, who encouraged him in this course, he wrote pointedly:

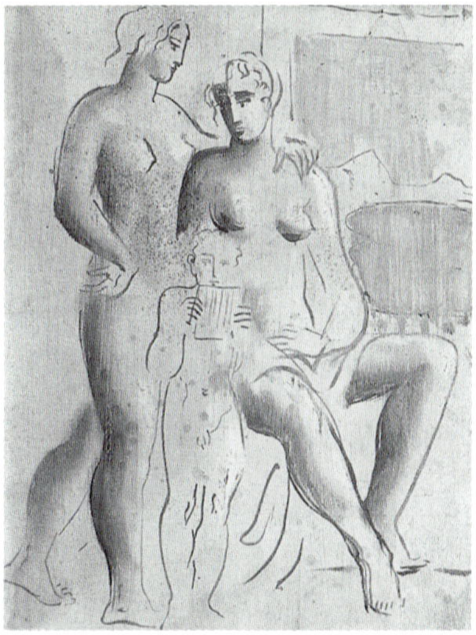

fig.12 *Figure Group*, 1926, pen and ink and watercolour. Private Collection (EN 150)

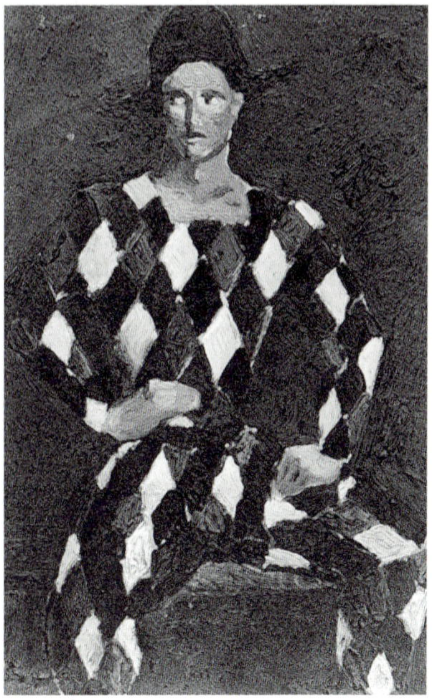

fig.13 *Harlequin*, 1925, oil. Private Collection (EN 69)

> You say then why not work for Molyneux designing silky clothes for silly women – a job like that would mean the end of everything. Is it your ambition to see my drawings in *Vogue* or *Tatler*? Perhaps it is, but it is not mine. My ambition as I said is to be a great painter and as I am learning now I shall stand every chance of becoming one. I'm going to see everything, think hard and read hard.[6]

Two meetings were to provide Wood with the right masters to lead him forward on his chosen path: Picasso and Cocteau. Each of these was indisputably the dominant figure in their respective artistic fields, and their example and support were to transform Wood's aspirations into reality. It was Gandarillas's aunt, Mme Errazuriz, in her time a celebrated hostess and one of the foremost collectors of Picasso's work, who introduced Wood to him at a dinner party. Noted for her beauty (her portrait was painted by Sargent), she was also remarkable for her culture (her conversation was compared by Cocteau to the writing of Montaigne). She was a great discoverer of new talent, and her patronage embraced all the arts, including music (Stravinsky), poetry (Cendrars) and architecture (Le Corbusier). She 'adopted' Wood, already by this time a great admirer of Picasso. And the master showed him favour, unexpectedly visiting his studio, giving him advice on the paintings there (despite his reputation for being stingy with praise), inviting Wood to visit him – all these attentions confirmed the young painter in his admiration and respect.

Contact with an artist of Picasso's calibre could hardly fail to impress a disciple still at the outset of his career. In imitation of him, Wood simplified his palette and learnt to be more sparing in his use of colour. He discovered from Picasso's example how the thick texture of household paint is malleable and can be effectively handled. His graphic work shows the master's influence; in his *Figure Group*, from 1926 (fig.12), he 'Romanises' the figures by giving them the heavy forms of classical deities, probably based on similar examples he had seen in Picasso's studio. In his first important exhibition, at the Beaux-Arts Gallery in London, the focal painting, a self-portrait, represented a stylish homage to Picasso, showing Wood dressed in a harlequin tunic (fig.13).

If he learned lessons in form and colour from the older painter, it was from Cocteau that Wood learned the art of drawing. According to the painter Francis Rose, the poet and Wood first met at the Hôtel Welcome in Villefranche on the French Riviera, where 'the lame and timid young man, with his strange English schoolboy's face'[7] came to lay before the 'prince of youth' some stage designs he had produced for a ballet to music by Lord Berners. These were very favourably received by the designer Bérard, who was also there at the time, and Wood was immediately taken up by Cocteau's circle. The fascination which the author of *Orphée* exerted on the talented and vulnerable youth of the time is well known. And for his part, the young painter fulfilled all the necessary criteria, being destined temporarily to fill the difficult void left in the poet's emotional life by the death of his writer friend Raymond Radiguet. Wood's slight limp qualified him for the Pantheon of 'limping angels', gifted young people whom the philosopher Maritain had accused Cocteau of 'devouring with a terrifying appetite'. It was this feature that Cocteau picked on in his poem 'Kit':

> This limp of his is puzzling in an angel,
> The weight of only one foot on the earth.

Everything about the writer captivated Wood, who wrote to his mother:

> Of course Jean like Picasso has the last word in good taste, and the two together have created the colour and the drawing and Cocteau the modern literature philosophy, and the modern school of music although he is not a musician … He is a God … One learns so much from his conversation, and realises that he is one century ahead of this century in his thoughts.[8]

In this unreserved eulogy, he left out only one thing – the importance of opium at this stage in the life of the poet, who, even if he wasn't responsible for introducing Wood to the drug, nevertheless gave it for him the seal of artistic respectability. One cannot underestimate Cocteau's influence, which was twofold – both positive and negative. A good judge and a fine critic, he handed out both encouragement and advice but equally, despite his own creative facility, extolled the virtues of practical commitment to a task, teaching by example. No one knew better than he the ins and outs of the Parisian art world and the importance of good publicity. He had influence, and used it to recommend Wood to Sergei Diaghilev.

In 1926 the impresario, whose inspiration was failing him, had planned to produce a 'cocktail version' of *Romeo and Juliet*, for the season at Monte Carlo. The project was to be thoroughly British, with music commissioned from a young prodigy, the twenty-year-old Constant Lambert. This project interested Cocteau, who had himself put on a 'modernised' version of the classic, for the soirées of the patron Etienne de Beaumont. Wood was asked to prepare the stage and costume designs for this new production and worked under the direction of Cocteau. It is in these sketches that one can see most clearly the poet's influence. They represent a ballet within a ballet taking place in a rehearsal room. In his drawings of male and female dancers resting, Wood adopts a distinctive technique of Cocteau's, using a continuous line that defines blank spaces, locks them inside its contour, and closes on itself. The line grows taut with the effect of flexed muscles or heavy with fatigue; profiles are clean, with eyes vacant, almost blind. As for the stage designs, these evoke the Hôtel Welcome whose theatrical character Cocteau often emphasised.

Almost as well known for his explosive quarrels as for his ballets, Diaghilev turned down the designs, or at least wanted to make so many alterations that Wood preferred to pull out of the project. Neither the intercession of Picasso and Cocteau nor Lambert's anger had any effect, and Diaghilev entrusted the execution of a simple backdrop to Max Ernst and Joan Miró (dubbed by Wood 'second-rate charlatans'), thus provoking what Ninette de Valois, who danced the role of the Nurse, has described in her memoirs as 'a theatrical scandal unequalled for noise'.[9] Once again Wood found himself – if indirectly – at the centre of a truly Parisian phenomenon, the opening night furore (in this case it was André Breton and the Surrealists protesting at the participation of *their* two painters in the *divertissement* of the elitist capitalist).

As far as his personal life was concerned, Cocteau considerably enlarged the young Englishman's circle of acquaintances. He introduced Wood to friends of his own age: the painter Francis Rose, a protégé of Gertrude Stein; the Surrealist writer René Crevel, whom Wood and Gandarillas were later to save from death by secretly nursing him in a hotel in Marseilles, following a pulmonary haemorrhage; musicians associated with the group Les Six – Georges Auric,

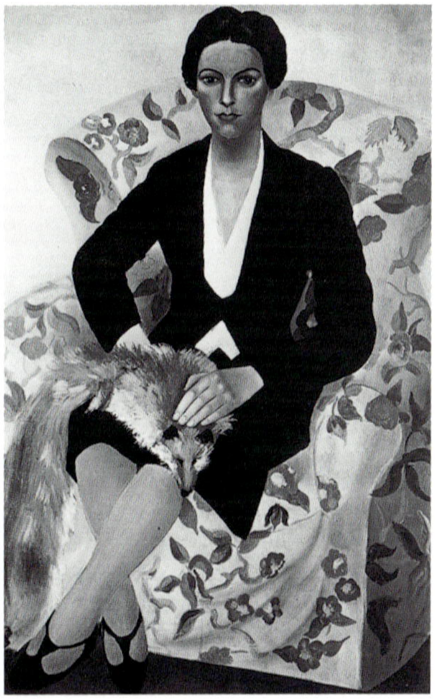

fig.14 *Mlle. Bourgoint*, 1929, oil. University of Sussex (EN 370)

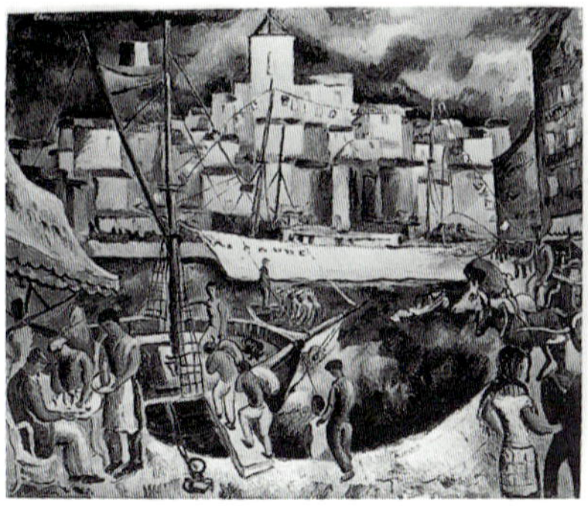

fig.15 *Marseilles Harbour*, 1927, oil. Private Collection (EN 248)

Francis Poulenc and Henri Sauguet; and other rising stars of the artistic scene. It was also Cocteau who put Wood in touch with Jean and Jeanne Bourgoint, the subjects of the best portraits he painted at this time (fig.14; no.5). The writer was to use their personalities and way of life as the basis for the eponymous *enfants terribles* of his novel. Jeanne, whom Wood considered to be the ideal model, became the partner of one of his first heterosexual affairs. In the letters he sent her – 'you are a wonderful woman; there's no one else who can make me feel the slightest emotion' – there is the suggestion, present also in the portraits, of a love nearer to friendship than to consuming passion. Her sleek body is perceived with a kind of detachment, neither sensual nor misogynistic. It is the body's contours rather than the flesh itself that holds the painter's attention. Wood's relationship with the young woman must have been fairly stormy, since Cocteau refers in a letter to the American writer Glenway Westcott to being 'worn out by Jeanne–Kit dramatics'. Jeanne, whom the poet had initiated into the use of opium, committed suicide a few months before Christopher Wood's own death, probably also suicidal.

Wood's frequent visits to the Côte d'Azur – to Villefranche, Canadel and Monte Carlo – were hardly conducive to painting. There were too many distractions for him there, and pressures too – for example, having to paint the portraits of rich Americans. And besides, the landscape did not inspire him. Not a single significant work survives from this period beyond a few watercolours and drawings – the best of these only pale imitations of Dufy, van Gogh or Matisse. Wood was himself dissatisfied with his oil paintings and destroyed most of those he painted in the French Midi. Only seaports, with 'their vibrant life, their humming, drumming activity' (Marseilles above all), seemed to him anything but dull. His paintings of these have a quality that looks forward to his later work (fig.15).

Between 1926 and 1928, the painter's turbulent personal life, his resentment of Diaghilev and disappointment in love, provoked his temporary return to England where he went in search of his roots. There he established himself in the London galleries that were showing work by younger artists, and his name appeared more often in the pages of art magazines than gossip columns. Cocteau had written a preface for his first important show, at the Beaux-Arts Gallery in 1927, pronouncing definitive praise: 'Christopher is without malice', ran his piece, 'An openness, a naïvety a purity of the young puppy who still hasn't caught the ills (or evils) of the age'. He concluded: 'Wood is an English painter; his work is reticent, it takes exercise in the fresh air'.[10] This impression was echoed by the English critic Peter Spencer Churchill, writing in the *New Statesman*:

> He has been influenced greatly by modern French work, but has not been conquered ... The dry winds of the continent have blown away from his canvases some traces of the fog that besets these islands, but they have left a clean colour and gay humour which is essentially English.[11]

This seems to show us how the different influences have been assimilated, how the alchemical fusion of imitation and originality has worked. It was at this turning-point of his life that Wood's ambivalence asserted itself. The rediscovery of the Cornwall of his ancestors, the meeting with the self-taught 'primitive' painter Alfred Wallis, the artistic debates that informed and inspired his

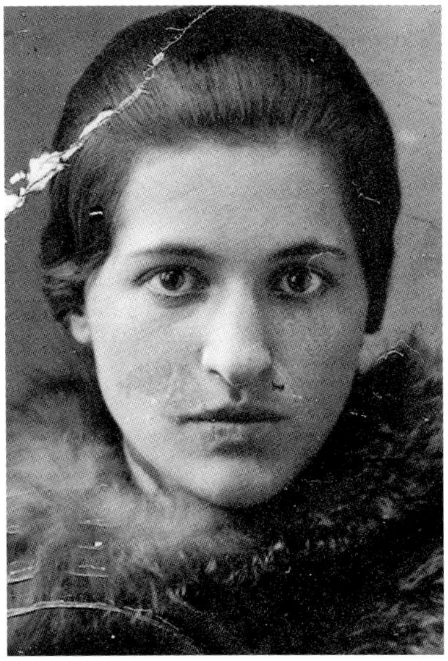

fig.16 Froska Munster, 1925 (TGA 723)

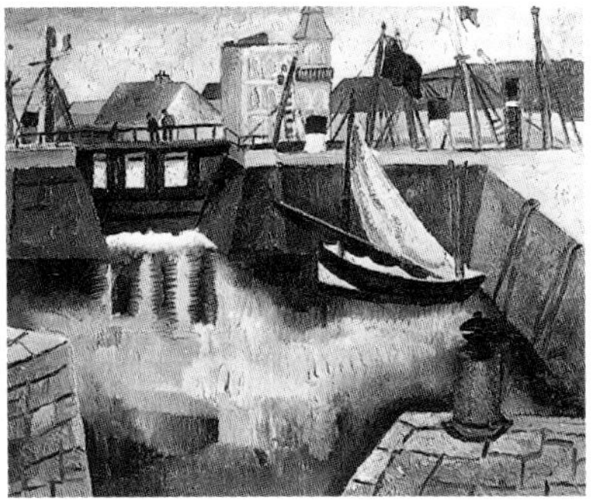

fig.17 *Harbour, Dieppe*, 1929, oil. Private Collection EN 350

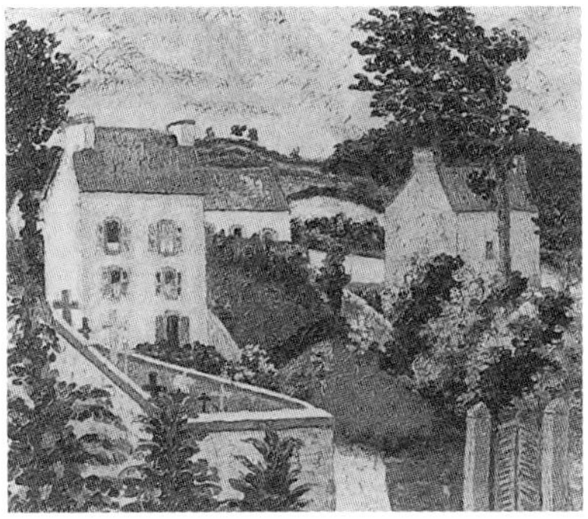

fig.18 Cedric Morris, *Corner at Tréboul, Brittany*, 1927, oil. Private Collection

friendship with Winifred and Ben Nicholson – all these elements, a blend of raw impressions and restrained sophistication, worked alongside and reinforced the influences experienced in France.

It was the need to prepare enough pictures for a forthcoming exhibition that took Wood to Dieppe in 1929. He was accompanied there by his new mistress, the young Russian émigré Froska Munster, friend of Bérard and Cocteau. A quiet, cheap hotel, the Hôtel Aguado, fine houses, large numbers of interesting-looking boats – in Wood's own words ' the most perfect happiness' – provided the conditions for new paintings that were remarkable both for their compositions and their austere colour scheme, in greys and blacks (fig.17). Froska Munster was well aware of the progress taking place; she wrote to Nicholson: 'Kit is working frantically, never puts his brushes down, strolls along quaysides looking delightedly at the boats. It sometimes bothers me that I'm the only critic to see his masterpieces.'[12] The artist's evident pleasure in what he saw, and the sense that he could now paint instinctively, freed him from any need to use models. Christopher Wood had become an intuitive painter, with a self-confidence that was soon to show itself in Brittany.

There had been numerous reasons behind this visit. Wood was hoping to get away from Paris so that he could work, attempting to sober up by setting some distance between himself and the world of Gandarillas and opium. He also wanted to conceal his affair with Froska, a married woman, from the prying eyes of the *beau monde*. For the purpose of living cheaply, like 'runaway lovers' as Max Jacob described them, Brittany with its modest family *pensions* was ideal. The region had also attracted Wood's attention through other painters of his generation who had spent time there in the early years of the century – Matthew Smith, Nina Hamnett, Cedric Morris (fig.18) and Frances Hodgkins. As Wood wrote to Nicholson: 'I want a very simple and light room, anywhere that is fresh and a bath and a few paints and one or two people I care for. I have no more ambition and I am bored by the old comfort.'[13] One could add that he was looking for a particular kind of sturdy fishing boat with brown sails that he had seen forced by storms into the Cornish ports and with whose crews he had chatted. Yet he was to be disappointed: despite the picturesque qualities of the seaside resorts of Dinard and St Servan, where he went in mid-July 1929, these places failed to satisfy him. On one hand, he discovered there the same fashionable Parisian set he was trying to escape from; on the other, the surrounding countryside struck him as a bland version of Cornwall. And there was hardly a fishing boat to be seen. Then one day, as he wrote to the Nicholsons:

> As we came round the corner there I saw about six of these lovely boats, lying quietly there being washed and refitted … I saw two go off. Up went their huge sails and they slipped off without a sound and by the time I got on to a little hill to see them again they were out to sea miles away. The sailors' wives, all dressed in black with white caps, sat all together in a small rowing boat and waited.[14]

These lines contain the first suggestions of a number of scenes Wood was later to paint, featuring sturdy trawlers, sometimes calmly riding the sea, at others engaged in a life-or-death struggle with the elements, with the sailors looking more at ease on their vessels than on dry land, handling the ropes with the grace of dancers. These subjects take us to the heart of Wood's painting around

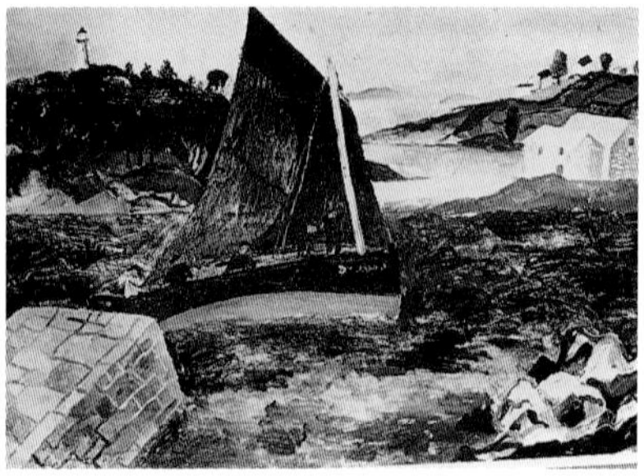

fig.19 *Boat Entering Harbour, Brittany*, 1929, oil. Private Collection (EN 371)

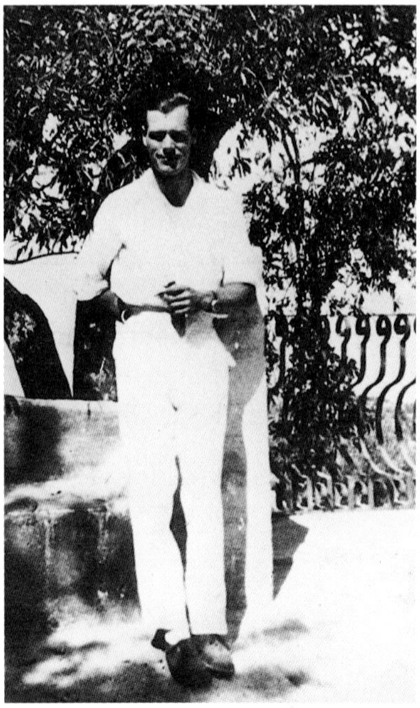

fig.20 *Christopher Wood at Tréboul*, 1929 (TGA 723)

the time of his two trips to Brittany during the summers of 1929 and 1930.

At Dinard Wood had been joined by Bérard and Pierre Colle, a young art dealer and friend of the poet Max Jacob, whose family owned a house near Douarnenez. This area of Brittany had been described to Wood as quite 'St Ivish'. He left Dinard with relief. At Douarnenez he stayed first at the Hôtel du Commerce, then rented with Froska a little house near the beach of Saint-Jean in Tréboul. He loved every detail of the place:

> It is quite new, absolutely simple, no carpets, white washed walls, a perfect W.C. Two charming bedrooms, a modern kitchen and a very pretty dining room with pale mauve doors going into a little garden with a big tree covered with purple flowers like lilac, and with hundreds of lovely butterflies living in it, then a garden which goes down to the sea where there is a little bay with lovely sand – there is a summer house under some trees where I sit and paint as all the boats coming out of the port pass the bottom of the garden and sail across the bay. It is a dream of quietness for me and wonderful for work.[15]

Jacob was himself staying at the Hôtel Ty-Mad, which he had punningly christened 'Ty Mad de Cocagne' (i.e. the land of luxury). The two men established a sincere friendship. Jacob focused on Wood the affection that the younger writer Maurice Sachs, his 'errant son', rejected; once again, Wood had discovered a homosexual mentor whose emotional needs he fulfilled.

In return, he received encouragement and genuine appreciation. Jacob wrote to Sachs: 'He's a great painter, very imaginative, very gifted, with a sure touch and able to conceive entire works that he executes quickly and confidently.'[16] Despite the difference in their ages, he and Wood found much in common: their recently reclaimed Celtic roots, a shared circle of friends, a certain whimsicality – more verbal than visual in the poet, but which also makes itself felt in Wood's gouaches of this time – and the same ideals in art. This last involved, in Jacob's words, painting 'simple works, without artifice or outmoded slickness, expressing things that have been felt and thought directly'.

Life at Tréboul during these summers of 1929 and 1930 was uncomplicated. The satisfaction of working side-by-side with a 'fellow labourer', as Jacob put it; weekends passed in the company of 'a young crowd' from Quimper, 'messing around with motor-cars, carefree and fragile',[17] including architects who taught Jacob the art of squaring up a painting from postcard-size, a lesson from which Wood also benefited – all this was a world away from the sophistications of the fashionable Parisian life-style he had been used to. Wood had hired a dinghy and – when he did not paint directly from nature – made drawings of Douarnenez and Tréboul that he worked up in oil paintings. He used household paint thinned with turpentine; and during the six weeks of 1930 which he spent at the Pension Cariou and Hôtel Ty-Mad, he almost regularly produced two pictures a day, which he propped up to dry all around the two rooms he had rented at the hotel. By contrast with his St Ives paintings, where the sun rarely shines, some of these Breton works radiate a deep sense of well-being, expressed primarily through the figures, caught in their ordinary daily activities with insight and sympathy – whether a Breton fisherwoman mending a net (no.29), women decorating the chapel of Saint-Jean, or sailors dancing (no.28). Wood had no need to go outside Tréboul, where he found more than

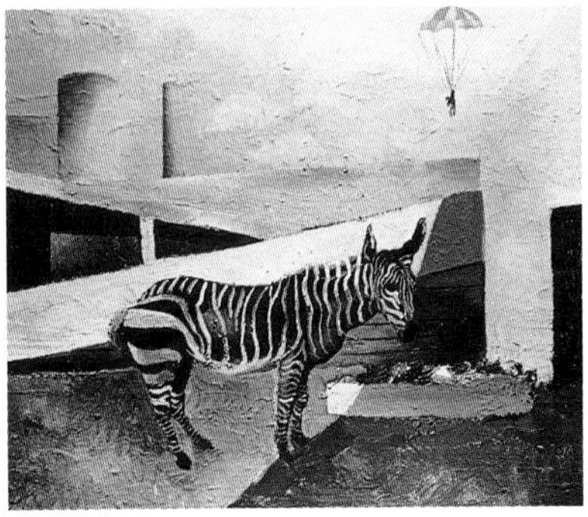

fig.21 *Zebra and Parachute*, 1930, oil. Private Collection (EN 409)

enough subjects for his paintings: the architecture of the white or grey houses perched on the hillsides; cypress trees tossing in the wind; a pink hotel (not Ty-Mad in fact, but Hôtel des Sables Blancs; no.21), chapels, and the town's shady streets and squares. Again and again, too, we see the fishing boats with brown sails, ploughing through a sea that is sometimes turquoise, sometimes an intense, deep blue, almost black – a sea which holds its mysteries and terrors, but which can also be gentle, breaking softly on a sandy beach. Max Jacob believed that a picture was the mirror of the artist's soul; and during these days at Tréboul, Wood swung dangerously between periods of intense happiness, such as he had hardly known before, and times of deep depression. His paintings and his letters to Froska (in which Wood always used this spelling of her name, although she also seems to have been known as Frosca) bear this out. He had not managed to break his addiction to opium, and, while the drug intensified his vision, it also unhinged his mind and sapped his strength. In early summer 1930, Jacob had described Wood to Sachs as 'the adorable Kit who hasn't a single fault'; now he was 'difficult to be around ... caustic bitter Pmocking'.[18] Cingria described Wood as looking white as a corpse, covered with opium ash, totally indifferent to a fire that had broken out directly under his window. Commenting on his indigo and violet seas, Winifred Nicholson wrote: 'The sea is not so much salt water, but the ebb and flow and depth of anguish.'[19] Dissonances and fractures characterise these works which are, with the exception of two paintings produced in Paris, the last he painted. They are vigorous, even coarse, in style, with the thick housepaint forced on to the canvas, remodelled and deeply scored with brushmarks. Both the method and the details of the composition mean that the viewer cannot help but take in the space around the painting itself. This crude quality represents less an inherent naivety than a return to the spirit of childhood, a simplicity that Wood took from Brittany itself, whose life and landscape are necessarily falsified when painted in a precise, mannered style. Wood offers us his impressions, his delights, spontaneously and fresh as they come, with hardly any reworking. 'Genius – it's having understood the world before having lived in it', wrote Jacob in his posthumous homage to Wood. One could equally say that it means painting the world directly, without the dessicating intervention of rationality.

The final phase of Wood's career in France, in August 1930, terminates with two paintings of the Paris where he had started out (fig.21 and *Tiger and Arc de Triomphe*, The Phillips Collection, Washington D.C.; EN 380). These are clearly influenced by Surrealist art, signalling both a backwards glance and a new departure for Wood, who had from time to time brushed the edges of this movement without ever engaging fully with it. There was to be no new departure beyond that of his sudden suicide that August – a Surrealist departure in itself. All Wood left those faithful French friends who remembered him was the image of 'a restless, serious spirit that painted such individual and powerful life into pictures of the sea and boats under sail'.[20]

Notes

1 M. Sachs, *La Décade de l'illusion*, Paris 1950, p.131.
2 Letter from Wood to his mother (TGA 773).
3 C.-A. Cingria, 'Ossianide', 84, pp.10–11.
4 Janet Flanner, *An American in Paris*, London 1940, p.6.
5 Letter from Wood to his mother (TGA 773).
6 Ibid.
7 Sir Francis Rose, *Saying Life*, London 1961, p.58.
8 Letter from Wood to his mother (TGA 773).
9 Dame Ninette de Valois, *Come Dance with Me*, London 1973, p.117.
10 Jean Cocteau, preface to exhibition catalogue, Beaux-Arts Gallery, London 1927.
11 P. Spencer Churchill, article in *New Statesman*, 23 April 1927.
12 Letter from Froska Munster to Ben and Winifred Nicholson (TGA 723).
13 Letter from Wood to Ben and Winifred Nicholson (TGA 8618).
14 Ibid.
15 Letter from Wood to his mother (TGA 773).
16 Letter from Max Jacob to Maurice Sachs. Bibliothèque Classée de la Ville d'Orléans.
17 Letter from Max Jacob to Henri Ferrare, 20 June 1930. *Publication de l'Université de St Etienne, Centre de Recherche Max Jacob*, 1.
18 Letter from Max Jacob to Maurice Sachs. Bibliothèque Classée de la Ville d'Orléans.
19 Winifred Nicholson, preface to *Christopher Wood*, exh. cat., Arts Council of Great Britain, London 1979, p.6.
20 Charles Gilbert, *Le Petit Journal*, 17 May 1930.

Postcards and Painting: The Case of Christopher Wood

François Steel-Coquet

Those familiar with the part of Brittany painted by Christopher Wood – Douarnenez and Tréboul at the tip of Finistère – will feel instant recognition when standing before certain of his paintings. On the one hand they display highly precise topographical realism, due to his reliance on postcards; on the other hand there are strange dissonances where the photographic authenticity is almost always disturbed by Wood's use of unexpected, original and incongruous elements.

Wood makes no secret of his borrowing. Writing from Tréboul to his friends the Nicholsons, he says: 'I painted a good deal of architecture and less boats for a change, and this seems to make it easier to make a quieter composition. I'm very amused by everything I see and I find the postcards of this country very helpful.'[1]

Throughout the course of his international travels he had always preferred letters, where he could pour out his feelings, to the brevity of a few lines scribbled on the back of a card. In Cornwall he began to adopt this latter form of correspondence, however, sending his mother postcard reproductions of landscapes and of nothing else. He does not seem to have used them for his St Ives paintings, perhaps because he could paint the view in front of him without even having to leave his house. (It is true he could also do this from his window at Ty-Mad, his hotel in Tréboul, from where he had a sweeping, but more limited view, down to the Saint-Jean chapel.)

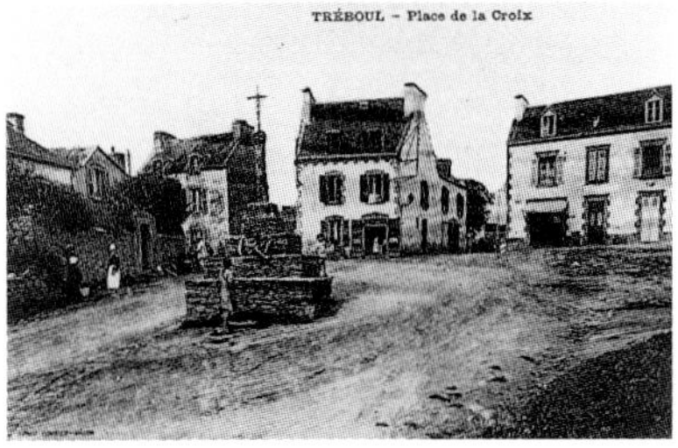

fig.22 Postcard of the place de la Croix, Tréboul

The postcard iconography that he found in Brittany was altogether different. In it he saw perspectives coinciding with his own vision, unaffected and spontaneous in approach. For between 1890 and 1930 a Quimper publisher had been collecting images of a whole way of life. Conscious of a disappearing culture, Jean-Marie Villard recorded not just picturesque Breton landscapes on postcards, but also a multitude of local scenes: markets, fêtes, weddings and the daily round. A century on, this collection of ordinary human activities has become an ethnographic archive. Some of these images were the ones that Wood chose to send to his mother: *Wedding Couple at Ploaré Dancing the Gavotte; View of Douarnenez Harbour, Resting Sailors; Douarnenez Main Harbour with Returning Boats.*

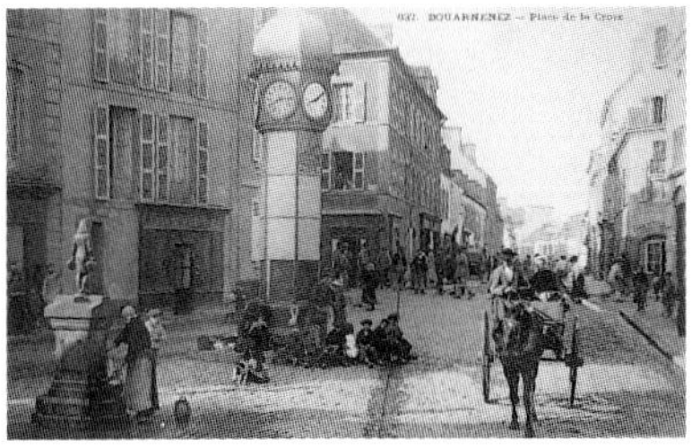

fig.23 Postcard of the place de la Croix, Dournenez

For painting purposes he made use of postcard views of the ports of Camaret and Concarneau, the streets and squares of Douarnenez and, in particular, rue Sainte-Hélène, la place de l'Horloge and the beach of Saint-Jean, scenes that were always peopled with diminutive figures. This borrowing procedure was not new, in particular in Breton schools of painting, because of the shared interest of painters and photographers in genre scenes and of the inspirational quality of local postcards. Good as the paintings sometimes were they nonetheless often had a superficial quality, characterised by a sort of frozen perfection. As we shall see, it was the essence of these places – places that he did not know well, but intuitively understood – that Wood aimed to capture. The cards helped him greatly in his work. The French poet Max Jacob, who happened to be staying at the same hotel and befriended him, must no doubt have drawn his attention to the pictorial potential of these photographs. Set to the task of producing gouaches 'for finance and food' or 'instant-gouaches, available in all good shops' as he ironically put it, Jacob was taking lessons in *mise au carreau*, or grid-scale enlargement, from young architects from Quimper who were weekending in Ty-Mad. The Swiss writer Cingria described the scene in his 'Propos': 'We were staying in a funny little hotel with the English painter Kit Wood and some young architects. Max needed them to enlarge the postcards that were the basis of his watercolours ... but mostly we spent the day laughing.'[2]

Both had to work fast; Jacob to get some income and Wood to finish enough paintings for his forthcoming exhibition. Why not then adopt this easy method of ready-made landscape? The previous year, at St Ives, the young English painter had joked about his pictures: 'I paint 'em two a day, cheap and nasty.'[3] Quality excepted, at Tréboul, recourse to postcards helped him maintain the same output.

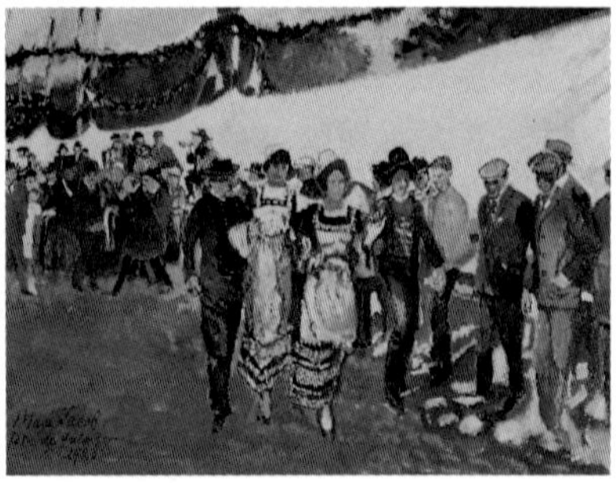

fig.24 Max Jacob, *Fête at Quimper*, 1925, gouache. Musée des Beaux-Arts, Quimper

Max Jacob's procedure with respect to his postcard method is well-attested. Among his card-inspired Breton pictures he concentrates on local festivals, the election of the queen of the Fête de Cornouailles, processions, dances and scenes with religious subjects. An enlarged drawing on the grid of a sheet of card, by him or by one of his 'helpers', formed the essence of the work – a few silhouettes and a sketch of the setting, after which it was a matter of reducing the scene to smaller dimensions again. Watercolour, gouache-pen drawing, pastel-gouache (a mixed media that he claimed to have invented) – the method varies. It may have taken a short time to complete, but the final result, in form if not in content, shows a close attention to detail of costume and posture, whose elegance is particularly accentuated in, for instance, *Fête at Quimper* (fig.24). The easily worked gouache effortlessly links the various elements of the scene, suggesting the vitality and rhythm of the dance. The photographic blur of the spectators' faces in the background is expressed in the painting by an absence of facial characteristics. Easy, bright effects punctuate the picture; for instance the flags, which are almost invisible in the photograph, are enlivened in red, white and blue. These are no longer quite the 'frail and transparent drawings', as Hélène Seckel described them, of the early gouaches Jacob did from Paris postcards in 1920. There is more solidity to them, less detachment and less easy charm and fancy.

If Wood thought of using photos in imitation of Jacob, his approach was altogether different. What he sought above all else was a solid architectural framework. Where Jacob suggests something with an outline, for instance Quimper cathedral in *Dancing in Quimper*, Wood faithfully reproduces the model, dwelling on the grey houses and banal squares of Douarnenez, as he had begun to do in Dieppe earlier in 1929. Each photographic image is a world in itself, the essence of which he distills. Transposing the grey-tinted cards, he comes close to Surrealism and to the thinking of André Breton, who saw in postcards messengers of a reality hidden from the world, capable of replacing literary description. Without use of the grid method, Wood could grasp the photographic image and project it directly onto the canvas. His knowledge of architecture allowed him to forego the intermediate step and the picture thus gained in spontaneity. While respecting the original angle of the camera, the proportions and perspective that it enforced, the painter appropriates the original postcard picture by introducing variations such as subdued notes of colour. He adds discreet reds and blues to the monochrome of *Douarnenez, Brittany* (no.19), and replaces the people massed at the foot of the clock. Where the photographer had frozen reality, the painter introduces movement. Windows also sometimes disappear, walls made blind like the featureless faces of the human figures.

For the painting based on the postcard of the rue Sainte-Hélène, topographically extremely faithful to the original (apart from the shop signs, the wall advertising and the figures walking along the street), Wood has only kept the Douarnenez woman seen from behind on the left of the scene (fig.26; no.24). He has obviously attempted a pictorial transposition of the grey shades of the postcard and of its slightly menacing shadows and neutral light, challenges which scarcely arise in today's technicolour age. The drab sky, a dirty white, remains as close as can be to the original. Thus all the transpositional technique concerns colour; spatial elements may have been taken out, but nothing has been added.

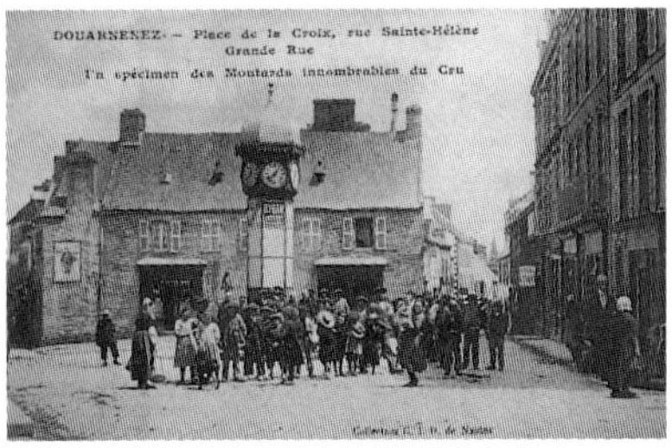

fig.25 Postcard of the place de la Croix, rue Sainte-Hélène, Grande Rue, Douarnenez

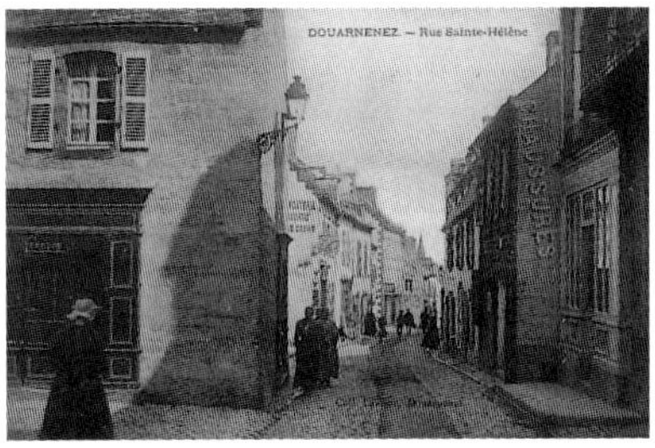

fig.26 Postcard of rue Sainte-Hélène, Douarnenez

For Wood this is unusual. More often, he uses the postcard as a background to which he adds imaginary elements. Sometimes the title of the picture does not correspond to the place represented, which intensifies the discrepancy for those who are familiar with the location. *The New Boat, Tréboul* (no.30), for instance, combines a representation of the Fort Vauban at Camaret (fig.27) that is accurately reproduced (and which Wood probably never visited) with a skeleton of a boat being built, the same boat that is at the centre of *Building the Boat, Tréboul* (no.37). In both cases a cliff topped by houses occupies the distant perspective.

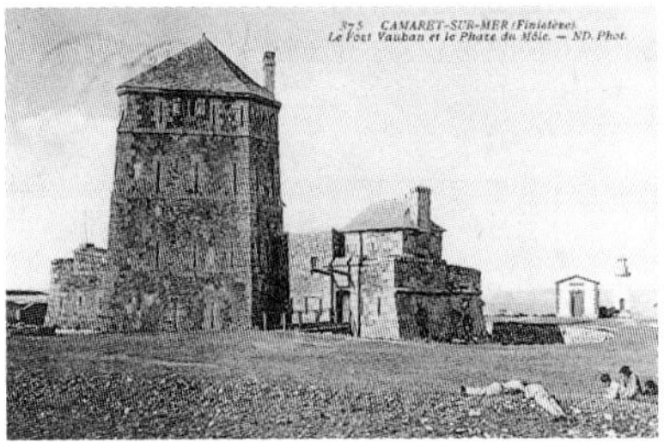

fig.27 Postcard of Fort Vauban and the Môle Lighthouse, Camaret-sur-Mer

As to the work known as *Sleeping Fisherman, Ploaré* (no.26), which is in fact set not in Ploaré but on the beach of Tréboul, the development of the painting is explained by the painter himself. On the back of a postcard of the plage Saint-Jean (fig.28) he jotted the following notes in French:

> Village le soir / Paysage très tendre, presque
> invisible, le ciel du soir gradé [sic] de vert pale.
> j'aime
> La maison du devant très éclairée les autres
> sombres dessinez [sic] beaucoup plus grand et plus simple
> que dans le [sic] photo.[4]

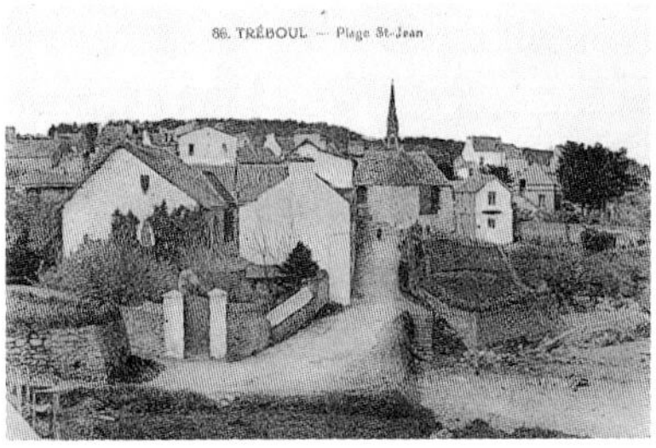

fig.28 Postcard of the plage Saint-Jean, Tréboul (TGA 8616)

With the landscape actually before his eyes, it seems that the painter has compared his own perception with the card picture, since his notes show every trace of the spontaneous. He also imagines what use he can make of it. It is only later that he incorporates these elements into at least two pictures, *Tréboul* (no.18) but especially *Sleeping Fisherman*. In the execution of this latter work he takes account of the simplification he mentioned. Whilst the lay out of the beach conforms to reality and to the postcard, the architectural features – the church and the houses – have a symbolic presence. Strangely, the balance of the whole is broken by the presence of the sleeping sailor, drawn if not painted in the style of Cocteau, and out of proportion, since it takes up nearly a quarter of the space. The sailor's quasi-mythological appearance is another incongruity. It is these multiple tensions which make this picture a particularly arresting one, with its grafting of personal elements onto the neutral background derived from the picture postcard. Even if the artist is borrowing another's image, in doing so he is far from absent from the one he himself is creating out of it.

It is hard to say whether this process is intentional or not, but it is frequent in Wood's painting. Realism, the order of the setting, is called into question by the introduction of discordant elements or by the simultaneous and almost conflicting use of different techniques. In *Sleeping Fisherman*, the crude features in the landscape contrast with the finesse in the drawing of the figure.

Why, on the one hand, this concern for truth, which leads Wood to copy cards and, on the other, this intrusion of displaced objects or figures, quite in keeping with the spirit of another aspect of Surrealism? Certainly, a slavish copy of a photograph would be of little interest and a denial of creativity. The model has to be reinterpreted if only spatially. In its dimensions the painting takes a middle road between reality and the reduced scale of the postcard. This twofold exercise of reduction and enlargement cannot but interest a painter, especially if, as is the case with Wood, he has studied architecture and moreover has worked on theatre sets, which demand a different scale again. Using postcards is yet another stylistic exercise. More prosaically, there is nothing handier for refreshing visual memories on rainy days. It is in this way that postcards came to complete the sketches Wood made of Douarnenez and Tréboul. In addition, working hard at his pictures by night, almost always under the influence of opium, which intensified his palette and filled his mind with visions, the recourse to these popular pictures provided a solid framework which stabilised him in his mental drift. On a realistic background he could give free rein to his poetic fancy.

It is true that these borrowings are similar to the pastiches he painted earlier in his career from the works of the modern masters, Cézanne, Picasso, Matisse – vestiges of insecurity here, perhaps; a desire for order, but an order which would not be so rigid that he could not anchor his own fantasies, phantasms even, on it. Paradoxically this stable foundation gave him greater freedom of expression.

The activity of Wood in Brittany was, above all, that of a spontaneous, intuitive seeker-out of images, seizing visual experience on the wing and transposing a banal reality, firmly rooted in its own vernacular environment, without any painterly preconceptions or retrospective corrections. The framework is borrowed, reworked and transfigured, and is always imprinted with his personal stamp.

It is in this way that the postcard, devalued and popularised by its endless distribution in time and space, becomes an element in the composition and the *aura* of a unique work of art. Nor does the cycle end there, since the work of art may itself, as Wood's works now are, be reproduced, desanctified and popularised in thousands of postcard copies.[5]

Notes

1 Letter to Ben and Winifred Nicholson (TGA 8618).

2 C.-A. Cingria, 'Propos' in 'Ossianide', 84, 1947–9.

3 Letter to Ben and Winifred Nicholson, quoted by William Mason in *Christopher Wood*, exh. cat, Arts Council of Great Britain, London 1979, p.28.

4 'Village in the evening / Very soft landscape, almost invisible, gradated evening sky pale green. I love it. The house in front very well lit, the others dark draw much larger and simpler than in the photo'. Wood's punctuation is as given in the text. He makes mistakes with his French, for example 'gradé' for 'gradué' and 'dessinez' for 'dessiner'.

5 Thus the account of Ralph Dutton's journey in Brittany, *Normandy and Brittany*, London 1953, is illustrated with numerous photographs, including four photo-reproductions of Christopher Wood's paintings, which are among his works most inspired by photographs.

Catalogue

Catalogue note

Titles and date order used here are taken from Eric Newton, *Christopher Wood* (1938). The list in Newton's book was made at the time of the 1938 exhibition of Wood's work at the Redfern Gallery, London, but differs slightly from the list compiled by Rex Nan Kivell in that exhibition's catalogue. Numbers prefixed by EN relate to the list compiled by Newton and are used to identify works referred to but not illustrated in this book.

TGA refers to Tate Gallery Archive.

Authorship of the entries is indicated in the following way:

AC André Cariou
FS-C Françoise Steel-Coquet
MR Matthew Rowe
MT Michael Tooby
SB Sophie Barthelemy.

1 **La Foire de Neuilly** 1923

Oil on board 75 × 99 cm
Towner Art Gallery and Museum, Eastbourne
[Exhibited in Quimper only]

This extraordinary early painting dates from Wood's first real concentrated period of work, over four months in Paris. It was at this time that he met Picasso, whose work at the time was dominated by his so-called neo-classical manner. *La Foire de Neuilly* (Fair at Neuilly) has a dream-like quality, with figures and surroundings that resemble a decorative frieze, achieved with a meticulous attention to the handling of the brush. It is painted on board, which allows a hard, flat surface. Aspects of this work presage Wood's links with figurative artists such as Cedric Morris, whom he was later to meet through the Seven and Five Society.

MT

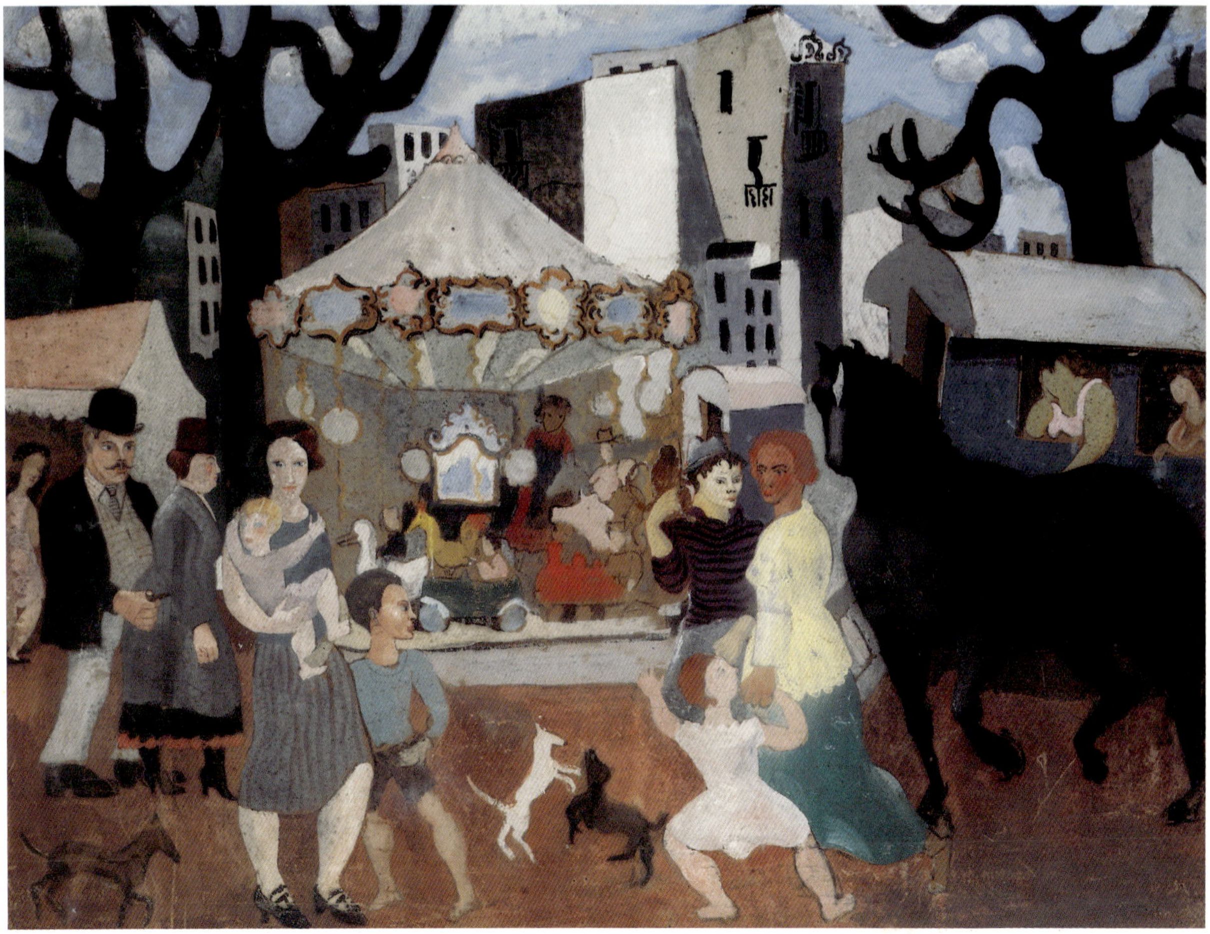

2 **China Dog in a St Ives Window**
1926

Gouache on panel 63.5 × 76.2 cm
Private Collection

Wood first visited west Cornwall on a touring holiday with his companion Antonio de Gandarillas in August 1926, visiting Penzance and the Isles of Scilly before deciding on St Ives as a place to stay. His decision to visit the area may have been influenced by his mother's Cornish ancestry but probably more immediately by the example of Cedric Morris, who had spent the previous summer in the area. Wood stayed at Pedn-Olva House in St Ives throughout September and October, remaining on alone after Gandarillas's departure at the end of the first month.

China Dog in a St Ives Window presents a view from one of the rooms out over St Ives Bay, behind a still life of a china figure group balanced on a strikingly coloured armchair. The choice of composition betrays Wood's artistic sophistication acquired in the studios of Paris, but the subject matter – a Staffordshire ornament and an austere steamer – reveals an interest in the quirky, parochial, rustic nature of Cornwall. The romantic tone of this painting is heightened by Wood's manipulation of the view in bringing forward the dramatic Godrevy Lighthouse perched on its own small island.

MR

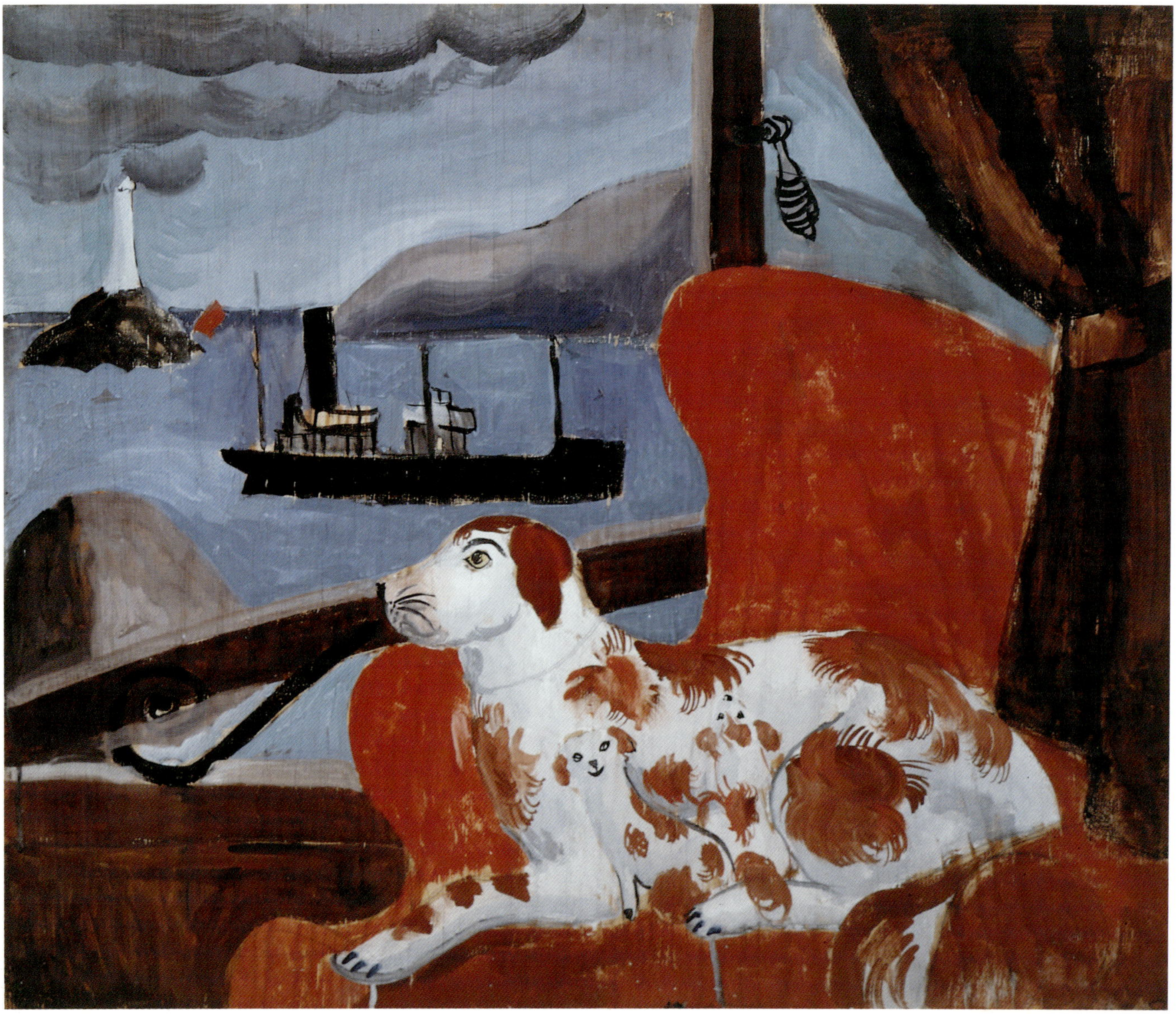

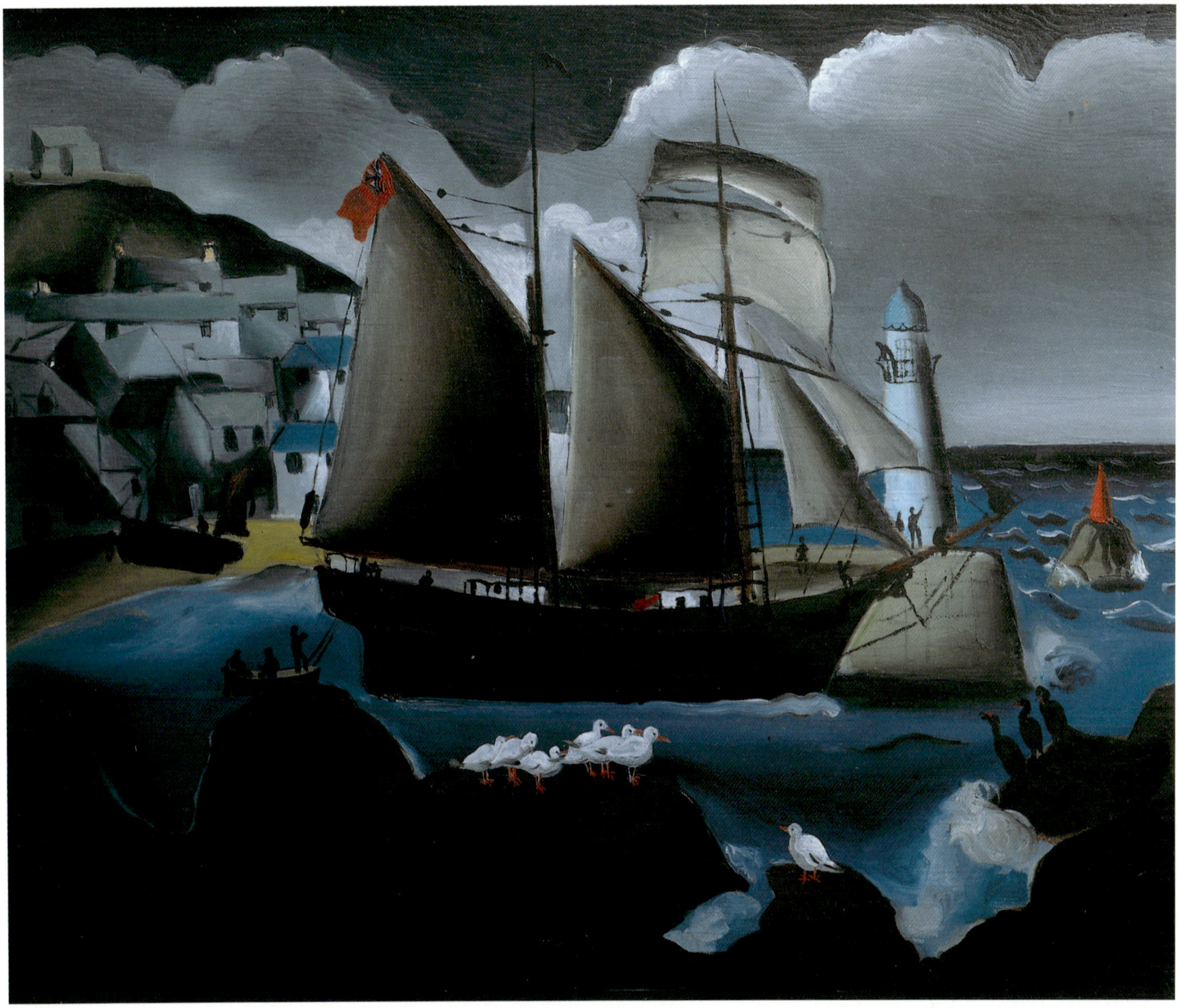

3 **Ship Leaving a Cornish Port** 1926

Oil on panel 63.5 × 76.5 cm
Private Collection

In a letter to his mother dated 6 September 1926, Wood described how a window of his house in St Ives looked 'onto a few rocks where the sea is always up as the tide only changes a foot or two. Opposite is the little port, full of fishing boats, and the little grey houses go up and up behind it and are topped by a little green hill with a small chapel on it, which adds greatly to the interest of the composition. There are two lighthouses and the old quays run around the harbour' (TGA 773).

In *Ship Leaving a Cornish Port*, Wood uses this view as the backdrop to his composition. The large, antiquated sailing boat appears to be out of scale with the rest of the scene, as if dropped in from elsewhere. Indeed, with its full sails hoisted while still within the harbour it lends the painting a fantastical, dreamlike quality. This is heightened by the dark, restricted palette, which suggests a night scene.

MR

4 **Loading the Boat, St Ives** 1926

Oil on canvas 50.8 × 60.1 cm
Manchester City Art Gallery

This image is more likely to be based on Wood's memory of the harbour at Penzance than a direct view of St Ives. Wood had stayed in Penzance for a few days in August 1926 before moving to St Ives, and towards the end of September travelled around the area extensively by car. The metal bridge that cuts the painting horizontally displays similarities to the original Ross swing bridge or even to the narrow walkway above the harbour gates at Penzance. It may also make reference to the railway viaduct in the nearby town of Hayle, which would explain the inclusion of the houses visible through the bridge. The busy harbour scene, with its shirt-sleeved sailors, may refer to memories of Mediterranean ports that Wood had visited years before.

The overall rich tonality, highly textured surface and free-flowing outlines recall the work of Cedric Morris, whose paintings of the previous summer present a similar impression of a hardworking, earthy Cornwall.

MR

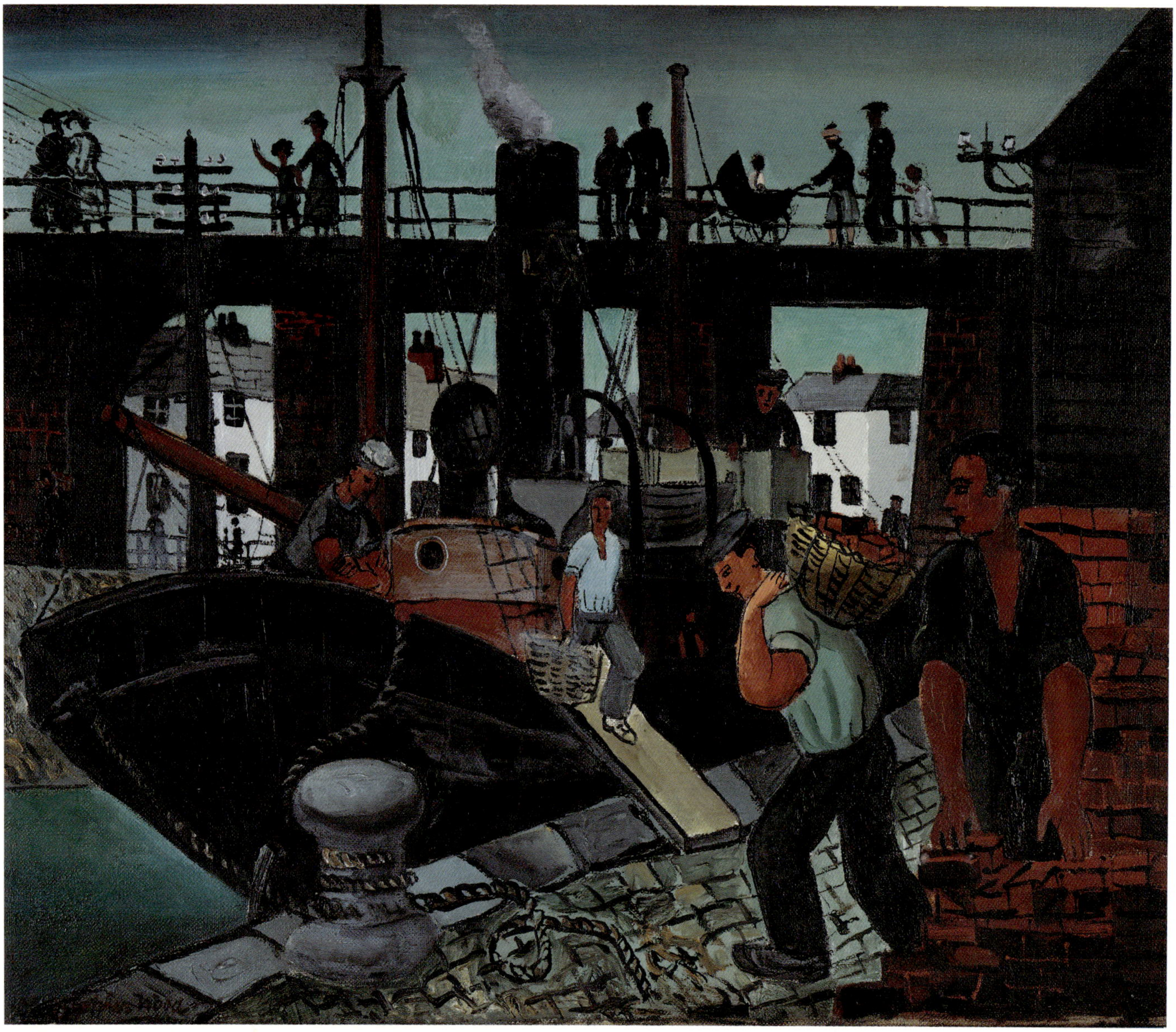

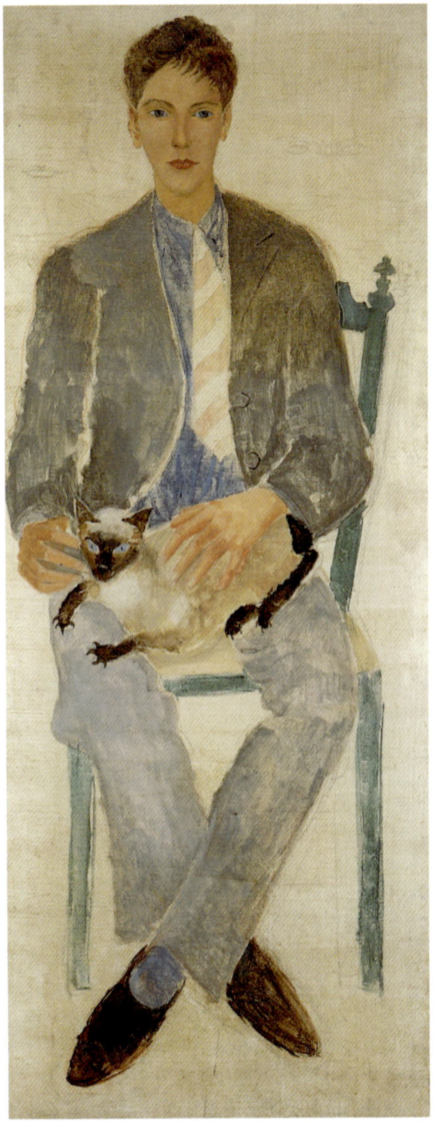

5 **Jean Bourgoint with Siamese Cat** 1926

Oil on paper 149.2 × 54.6 cm
Kettle's Yard, University of Cambridge
[Exhibited in Quimper only]

Wood met Jean Bourgoint in 1925. Like Wood, Bourgoint was one of Jean Cocteau's circle, and was introduced to opium by Cocteau. Members of this circle, which shifted between Paris and the Riviera, speculated at times that Bourgoint had supplanted Wood as the object of Cocteau's desire. Jean and his sister Jeanne were the models for the characters of Paul and Elisabeth in Cocteau's novel *Les Enfants terribles* (see p.17).

Whilst being uncharacteristic of his mature work, *Jean Bourgoint with Siamese Cat*, now known as *Boy with Cat (Portrait of Jean Bourgoint)*, is one of Wood's most powerful paintings. The boy's presence is frail yet full of energy. The cat's pose, with its outstretched claws, is emblematic of the balance between elegance and tension that Wood achieves. Even though the work appears unfinished, the details that reveal this – notably the alternative sketching technique used for Bourgoint's eyes and face – only serve to add to the painting's uncanny presence.

MT

6 **The Fisherman's Farewell** 1928

Oil on panel 27.9 × 70 cm
Sir Michael Culme-Seymour Bt

Wood returned to St Ives at the end of August 1928, in the company of his new lover Froska Munster, and the Nicholsons – Ben and Winifred and their son Jake – whom he had joined earlier in the month at Feock, near Falmouth, on the south coast of Cornwall. While on this visit to St Ives Wood and Ben Nicholson encountered the artist Alfred Wallis, an episode that has assumed an almost mythical status in the history of art in St Ives. By mid September Wood had taken a cottage in the town, near to where Wallis lived, with a view onto Porthmeor Beach; the Nicholsons rented a house set back from, but overlooking, the harbour.

While much has been made of the formal influence of Wallis on Wood and Nicholson, both artists' work had already displayed distinctly naive elements years before – Wallis represented more of a confirmation of their beliefs than a conversion. It would appear that it was the combination of the work and the man himself that impressed them. As a retired fisherman Wallis represented a certain Cornish integrity and directness that they admired.

The Fisherman's Farewell presents the Nicholson family in front of a view of St Ives harbour and bay. As Richard Ingleby has pointed out, the title may refer to the departure in October of Ben Nicholson, who left St Ives a few days before Winifred, to travel to London. By bestowing the title of fisherman on Ben, Wood reveals his esteem for his fellow artist, linking him with the people whom they both so respected. The sense of imminent loss is emphasised by the harbour behind the figures, which is cluttered with boats getting ready to depart.

MR

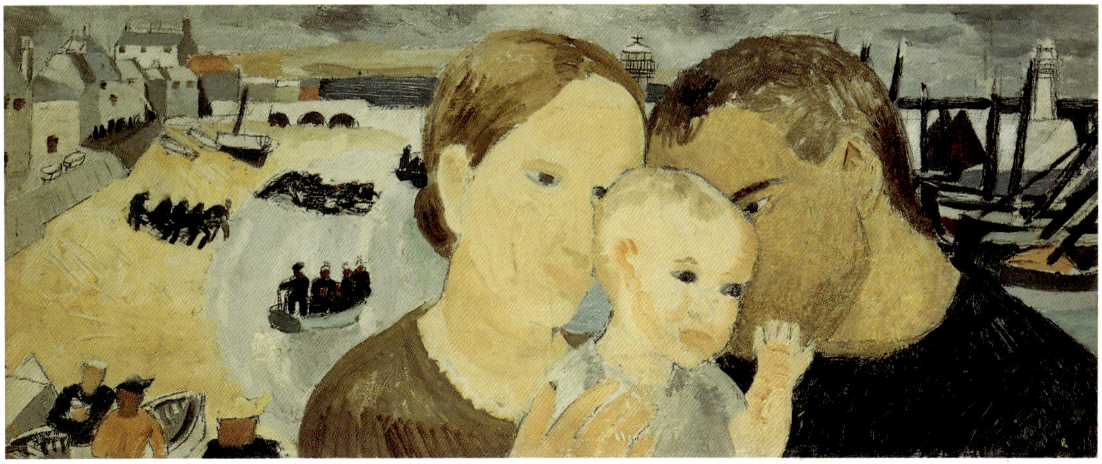

7 **Cornish Fishermen, the Quay, St Ives** 1928

Oil on canvas 63.5 × 76.2 cm
Aberdeen Art Gallery and Museums

By the end of October 1928, Froska Munster and the Nicholsons had all left St Ives. Wood stayed on alone until early December. This solitary period brought him closer to the people of St Ives, whose severe and often tragic existence he admired. The fishermen and their activities increasingly became the most interesting aspect of the port to Wood and informed the subjects of his paintings.

Cornish Fishermen, The Quay, St Ives is a view of the area of St Ives known as the Castle, a raised walled area above the entrance to Smeaton's Pier in the harbour. This area offered a view out over St Ives Bay and was popular with fishermen wishing to gauge the specific weather conditions. The building on the left, however, appears to have been drawn from the artist's imagination, perhaps prompted by a similar tall, narrow building that overlooks the path down to Porthgwidden Beach near the Island in St Ives.

The fishermen are portrayed in the centre of the canvas, full of dignity and importance, whereas the women are clustered inside the narrow building on the edge of the scene as if they feel uncomfortable or out of place in such a masculine setting. This view accords with Wood's description in an undated letter to Winifred Nicholson: 'St Ives is like a terrific roulette table at the moment. There is a terrific storm. The sea is dead white and angry white all over. The sea gulls and fishing boats are blown about like bits of paper and the women scuttle into their houses like frightened rabbits. The fishermen are heroes – they look like pirates with their big jack boots up to their thighs … they look very brave and dashing' (TGA 8618).

MR

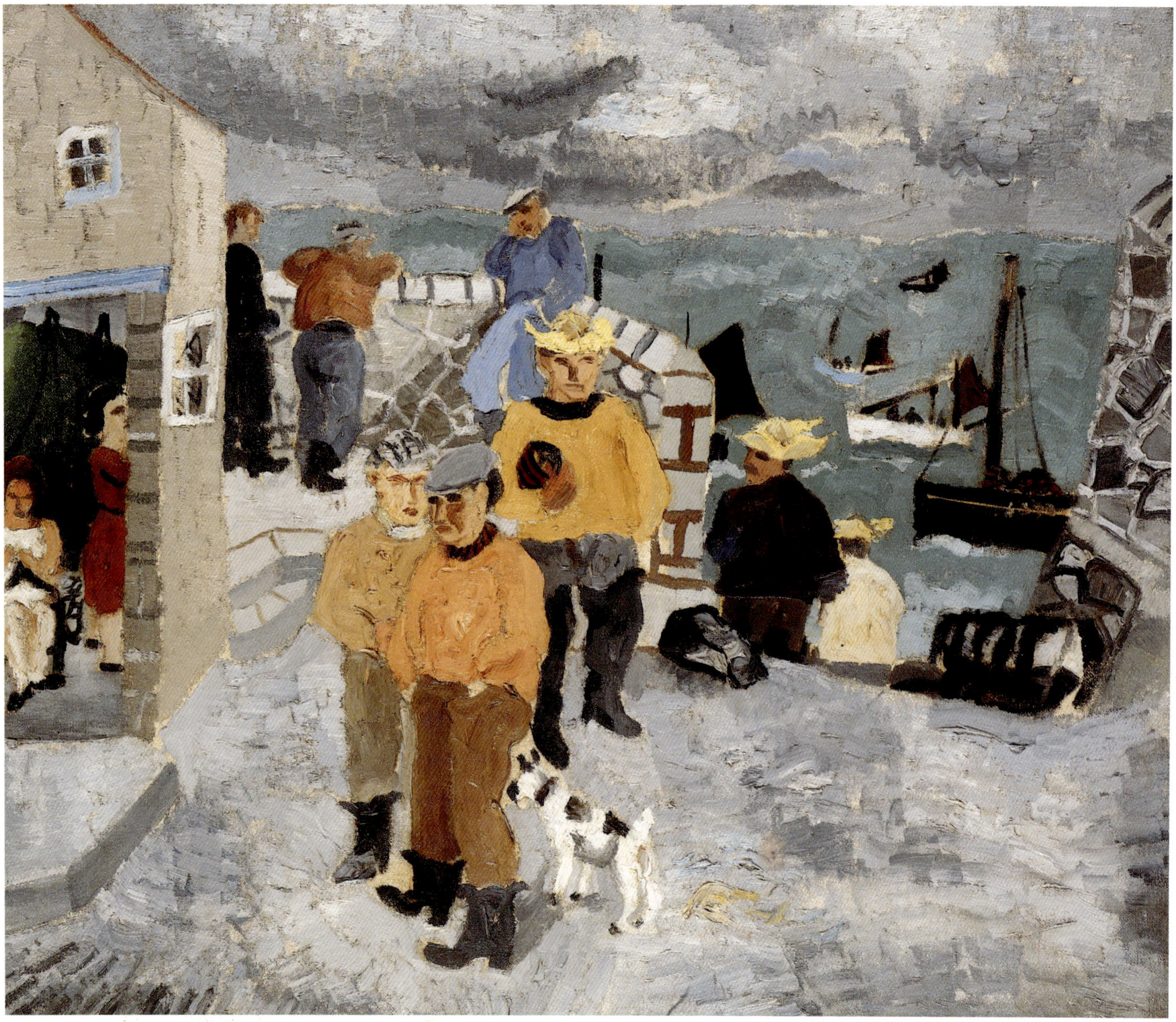

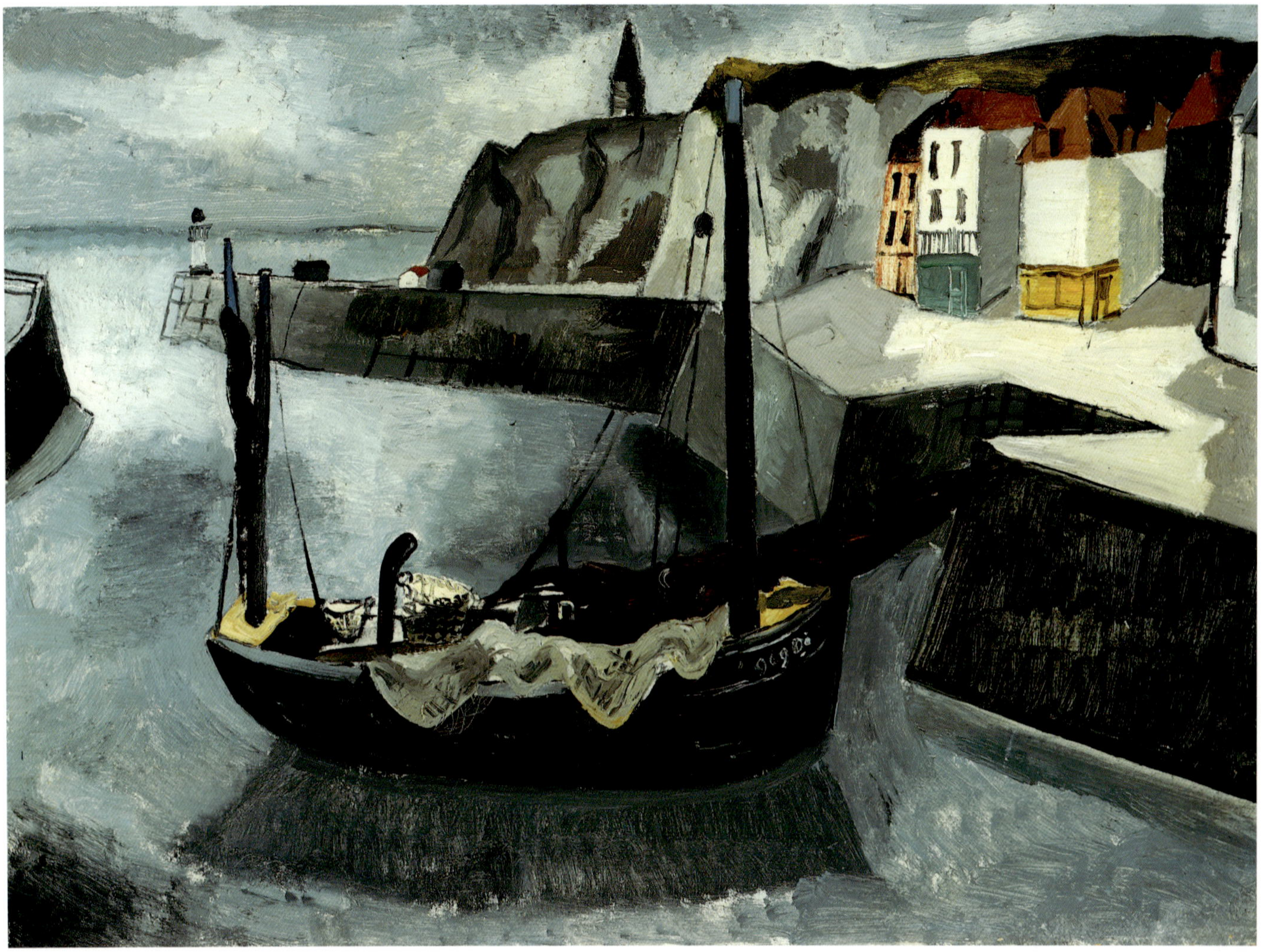

8 **The Quay, Dieppe** 1929

Oil on canvas 41.5 × 56.2 cm
Aberdeen Art Gallery and Museums

This is probably one of the best examples of Wood's bold use of so-called 'non-colours': grey, white, black and brown. He once wrote that 'no black is black enough', and certainly the various shades of black here show as many gradations in colour as in the yellow tones that theatrically light the landscape. The sombre tonality of the landscape suggests a menacing interlude between rain storms. The sky promises further showers, the sea is unusually still and the houses shuttered. A sense of threat hovers over the rain-washed quay, which seems strangely deserted.

FS-C

9 **Fishing-boat, Dieppe** 1929

Pencil on paper 32 × 40.7 cm
Aberdeen Art Gallery and Museums

After more than two years in England, where during his stays in St Ives he had been able both to rediscover his family roots and to develop a personal style, Wood returned to France, disembarking at Dieppe in April 1929. With him was his mistress, Froska Munster. Trying to avoid going back to Paris or the Côte d'Azur, and hoping to find a sense of solitude, Wood spent some time in this port. He was fascinated by the life of the harbour and the streets, of which he drew and painted several scenes. Observing his intense activity at this time, Froska recorded in her letters the painter's creative energy and new-found happiness.

In Dieppe, as in Penzance and later at Mousehole and Tréboul, much of Wood's work consisted of 'portraits' of boats, both drawn and painted. This careful drawing demonstrates both Wood's detailed interest in the way vessels were rigged and fitted out, and his desire to master the fundamental structural and spatial elements of composition. This is a preparatory drawing for the painting *Fishing-boat, Dieppe Harbour* 1929 (private collection; EN 356). For the painting Wood hardly changed the form of the boat itself (he added a couple of baskets and a rope on deck), but he integrated it fully into a complex interplay of lines, and colours values, creating a composition that is at once densely structured and rigorously simplified.

SB

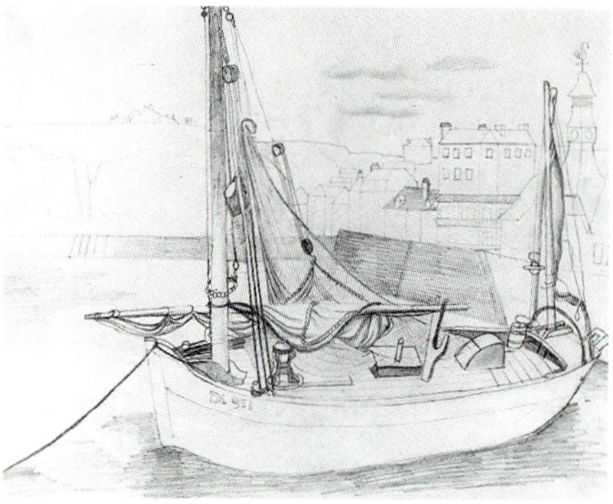

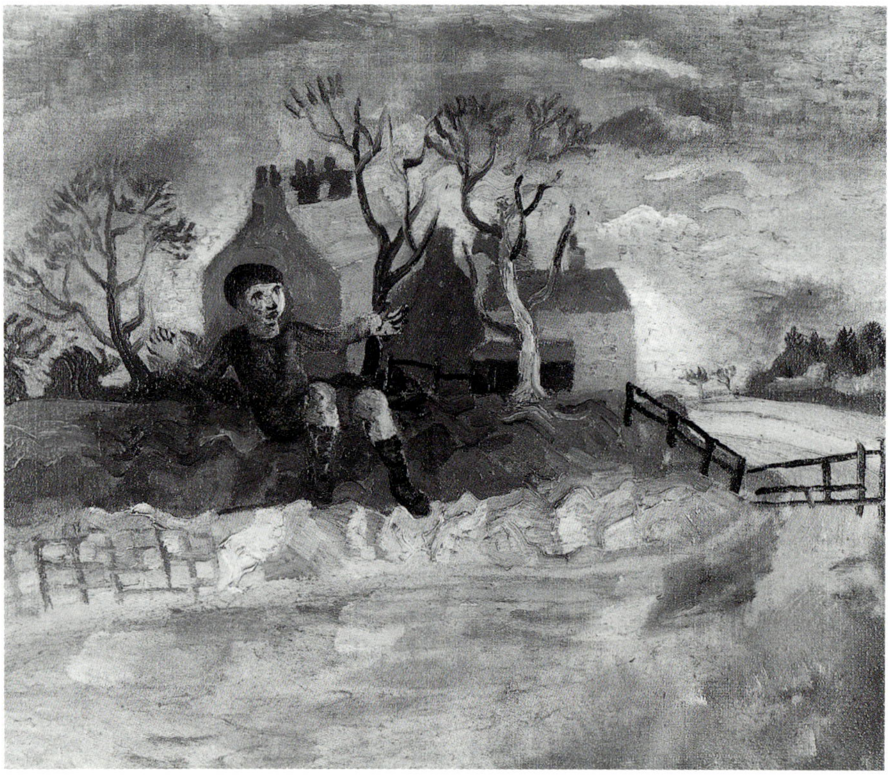

10 **The Jumping Boy, Arundel** 1929

Oil on canvas 45.7 × 54.7 cm
Sheffield City Art Galleries

Wood visited Arundel in Sussex briefly in March 1929. At that time he was suffering deeply from the symptoms of temporary withdrawal from opium, to which was he addicted. The picture was probably completed in London, and may be based on a sketch. It is a mysterious painting, in which the figure of the boy floats against the space of the compositional background of the picture.

MT

11 **Boat in Harbour, Brittany** 1929

Oil on board 79.4 × 108.6 cm
Tate Gallery, London. Presented by Mrs Lucy Carrington Wertheim, 1962

More like a portrait of a fishing boat than a representation of an actual place, this painting ranks among Wood's finest work. The port of Tréboul can be identified by the houses rising up behind the quayside and by the distinctive church steeple, but Wood has changed and added details. For example, the church is

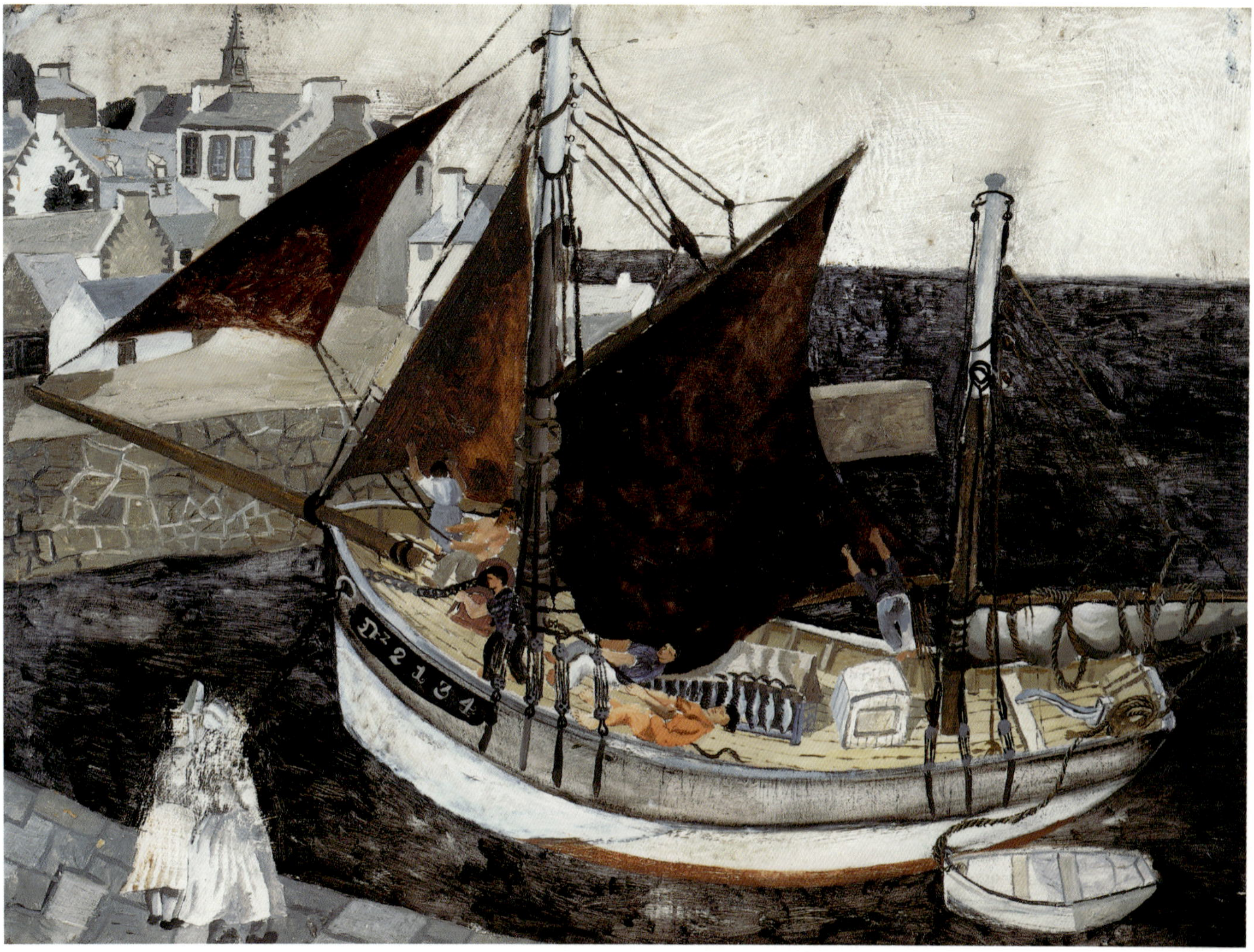

in reality further away up the slope to the left and the steeple is not visible from the far side of the harbour where the boat has anchored. The quay shown curving round in the foreground does not exist. In reality, the harbour walls extend some hundreds of metres along the shore of Tréboul; the harbour is not enclosed in the way Wood depicts it here. Nor does Wood show the edge of the Île Tristan, which should appear on the right. Here as in many other works, Wood's artistic preoccupations prevail over physical reality. He views the scene as though from mast height, which allows him to exploit an effect of diving down into the space, showing the boat's deck from above while simultaneously bringing it close.

Nevertheless, he has closely observed the delicate manoeuvre of bringing the boat into harbour, performed by the six sailors who are lowering the sail and dropping anchor. Two women, probably sailors' wives, watch from the quayside: one wears the *borléden* headdress worn by the peasant women in the countryside of the Quimper region, the other the *pen sardin* headdress of the women who worked in the sardine canneries of Tréboul and Douarnenez. These figures have been scratched out by Wood, and the picture may remain in an unfinished state, as it was acquired directly from the artist's studio after his death by his dealer, Lucy Wertheim.

Wood has carefully transcribed the code used to identify boats registered at Douarnenez, which includes those sailing from Tréboul. Gaps in the local maritime archives mean that we cannot know whether the boat's registration number corresponds to one that Wood may actually have seen.

Tréboul at this time was crowded with fishing boats, whose main catch was sardines. The boats jostled side by side the whole length of the quayside, and hardly ever dropped anchor in the middle of the harbour. Rather than show a boat at a quayside mooring, Wood makes a single boat take up the whole of the picture and constructs an evocative setting around it.

This work can be compared with other portraits of fishing boats painted at Penzance and Dieppe. It is striking evidence of Wood's infatuation with this kind of boat, which dates from his meeting with Alfred Wallis and his visits to Falmouth and elsewhere in Cornwall. He enjoyed sailing, and did some during the summer of 1929 at Tréboul. From an artistic point of view, he also loved the rounded forms contrasting with the clean lines of these colourful boats, the sails of which were of a marvellous brown colour.

AC

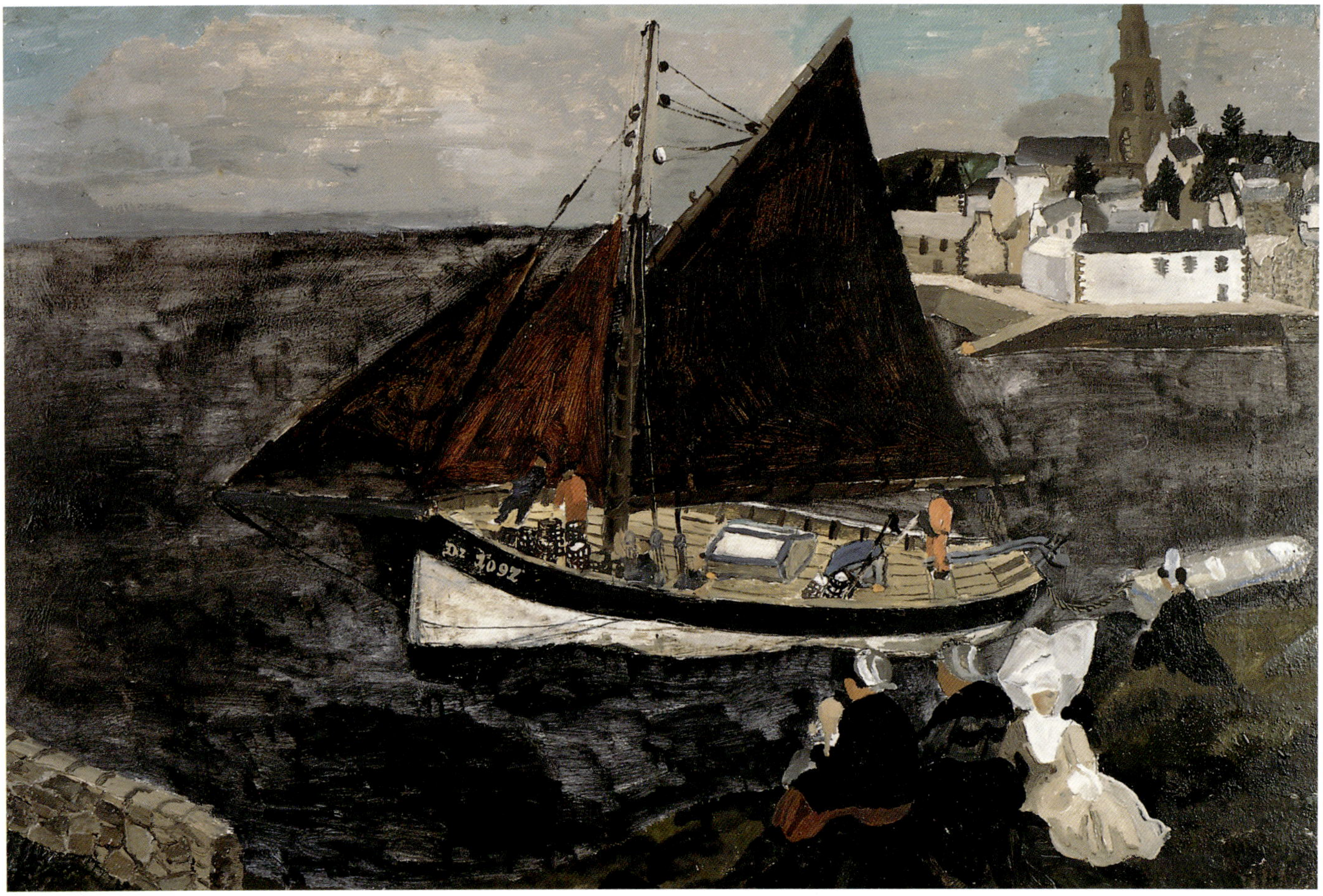

12 **French Crab-boat, Tréboul** 1929

Oil on board 51.5 × 78.5 cm
Towner Art Gallery and Museum, Eastbourne

A fishing boat with the registration number DZ 2092 sets sail from the Port Rhu. It is manned by a crew of three, and the deck is loaded with crab pots. In the background can be seen Douarnenez, the docks of Le Guet, the salthouse, a few houses rising up the hill, and the church steeple. In the foreground, four women are sitting on the headland of Pen-Ar-Vir at Tréboul. Three of them are in traditional dress: two wear the *pen sardin* headdress and one the *borléden*. They are looking out to sea, at the ship under sail; the one furthest to the left may be knitting. In contrast, a nun, dressed in white and wearing an impressive *cornette* (headdress) turns her back on the sea.

While this everyday subject, showing women by the coast, had often been chosen by painters at Concarneau, Douarnenez and Camaret, it was usually treated in a picturesque manner, with the women clearly waiting for the fishing crews to return, or shown as widows or young mothers with children, peacefully occupied at the harbour mouth or sometimes staring in anguish at the stormy horizon.

As with *Boat in Harbour, Brittany* (no.11), gaps in the local maritime archives make it impossible to know whether the boat's registration number shown here corresponds to one that Wood may have seen. However, it seems inappropriate to look for identifying details in this painting, which is more a generic 'boat portrait'. The little wall in the lower right is an invention of Wood's that he uses to close the composition, and this is balanced by the oblique line of the dinghy attached to the fishing boat. Wood has reduced the landscape in the background to its simplest elements – the few buildings shown bear no relation to their actual scale – and in this way enhances the effect of the sturdy church tower, the steeple of which Wood left unfinished.

AC

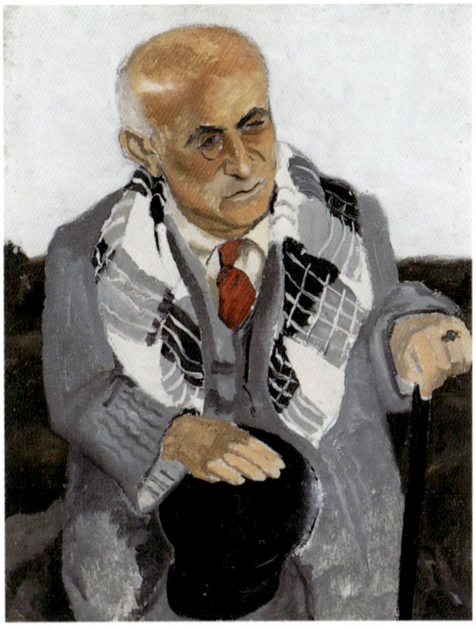

13 **Portrait of M. Max Jacob** 1929

Oil on canvas 60.9 × 50.8 cm
Musée des Beaux-Arts, Quimper

At the time this portrait of Max Jacob was painted Wood hardly knew the poet, whom he had only just met at Tréboul. Nevertheless, it demonstrates Wood's insight; the bitter crease in the corner of the twisted and almost cruel lips conveying 'a feeling of indefinable unease', as Picasso's companion Fernande Olivier remarked on a first meeting with Jacob. These characteristics are set down with a confident line, even if the proportions are awkward, with the head too large for the body. The choice of grey does not make the portrait in the least insipid; indeed its monochrome character gives it its strength and holds the attention.

FS-C

14 **Le Phare** 1929

Oil on board 54.6 × 80 cm
Kettle's Yard, University of Cambridge
[Exhibited in St Ives only]

This work was made on Wood's first visit to Brittany. Its title emphasises the French context, yet its content and method is the most powerful example of Wood's affinity with Alfred Wallis. The tilt of the boat as it turns in the flat wall of colour that denotes the sea is almost a pastiche of the work of the old St Ives fisherman artist. Even the support, a piece of old board, adds to the sense of the work as an act of homage. The newspaper that gives the work its title, *Le Phare* (The Lighthouse), is a deliberate recollection of the image of the lighthouse that figured in so many of Wallis's compositions, as well as in Wood's own work of the previous year. Wood sets this reference to a guiding light alongside the playing cards, used in other works of this time. Painted in France, this work clearly shows that Brittany evoked strong memories of Cornwall for Wood.

Acquired by H.S. Ede soon after Wood's death, *Le Phare* has for the last thirty years been displayed at Kettle's Yard in Cambridge, formerly Ede's home and now open to the public. Ede hung the work close to a painting by Wallis, aware of the emphasis that Wood placed on the importance of Wallis to his own development as an artist.

MT

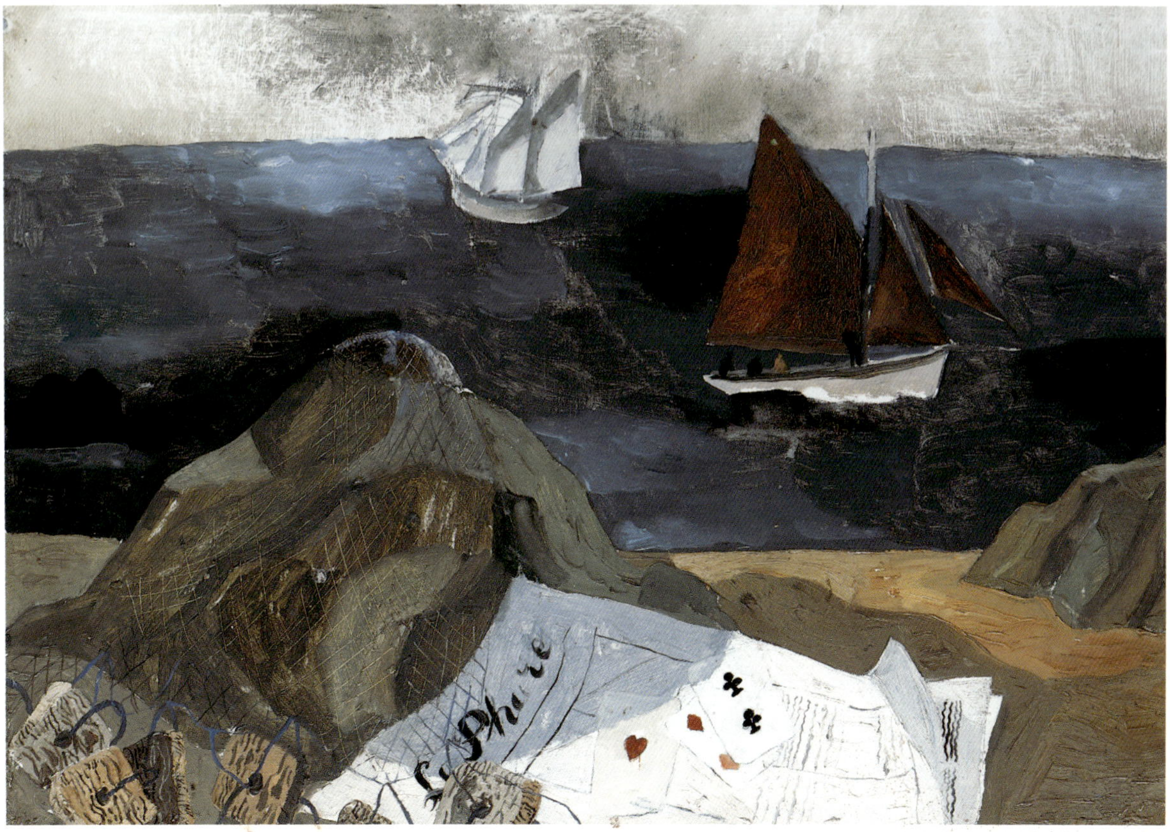

15 **The Manicure** 1929

Oil on canvas 152.7 × 101.5 cm
Bradford Art Galleries and Museums

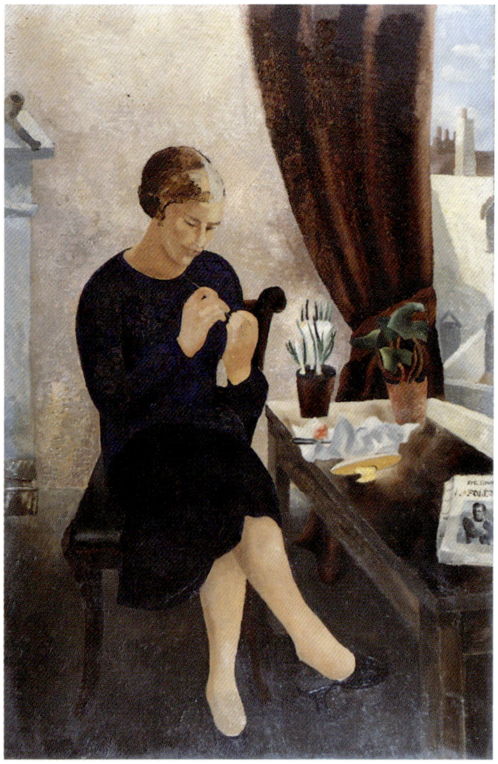

This intimate and informal portrait of Wood's mistress Froska Munster reveals the painter's feelings for her: to him she is a discreet and solid presence, secret and rather mysterious, who brings an absorption that he admires to everything she does. The density of the forms, simplified to the point of clumsiness, the muted palette, reduced to the artist's two favourite colours, blue and brown, all intensify the impression of security emanating from the young woman. Such a feeling is unusual in Wood's painting. The two pots of cyclamen and crocus are directly borrowed from a Winifred Nicholson picture.

FS-C

16 **Harbour Scene** c.1929–30

Pencil on paper 32.3 × 40.4 cm
Sheffield City Art Galleries

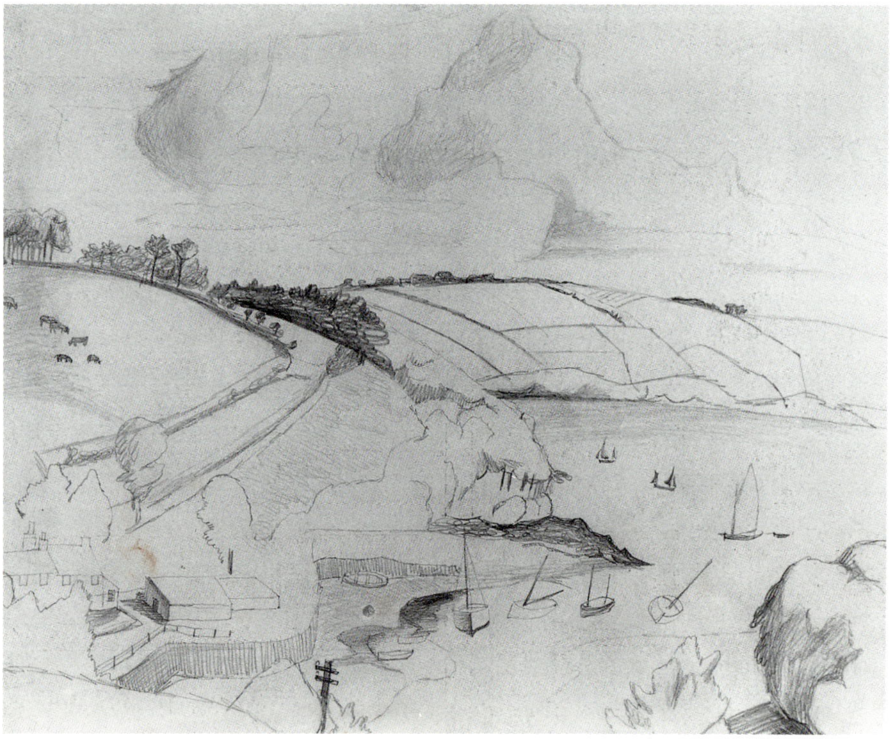

This drawing has tentatively been dated 1929–30, mainly because of the coastal location, which suggests a Breton scene, and because of the relative complexity of the composition in contrast to drawings made by Wood in 1928, during his visit to Banks Head, the Nicholsons' house in Cumberland. The level of finish is unusual in Wood's drawings and this appears to have the status of a work in its own right rather than being a study for a painting.

The effort that Wood has taken to record the specific details of the unidentified harbour illustrates the importance of this view to him and may be linked with his joy at finding similarities between Brittany and Cornwall during his first to Brittany in 1929. In a letter to Winifred Nicholson from Dinard he wrote, 'yesterday I went across to St Servan, a little port tucked away in a corner with wonderful grey houses with black roofs and round painted turrets and a beautiful fortress at its entrance. It is so quiet up a creek like St Mawes and as we came round the corner there I saw about six of these lovely boats lying quietly there being washed and refitted by their sailors in their red brown overalls' (TGA 8618).

MR

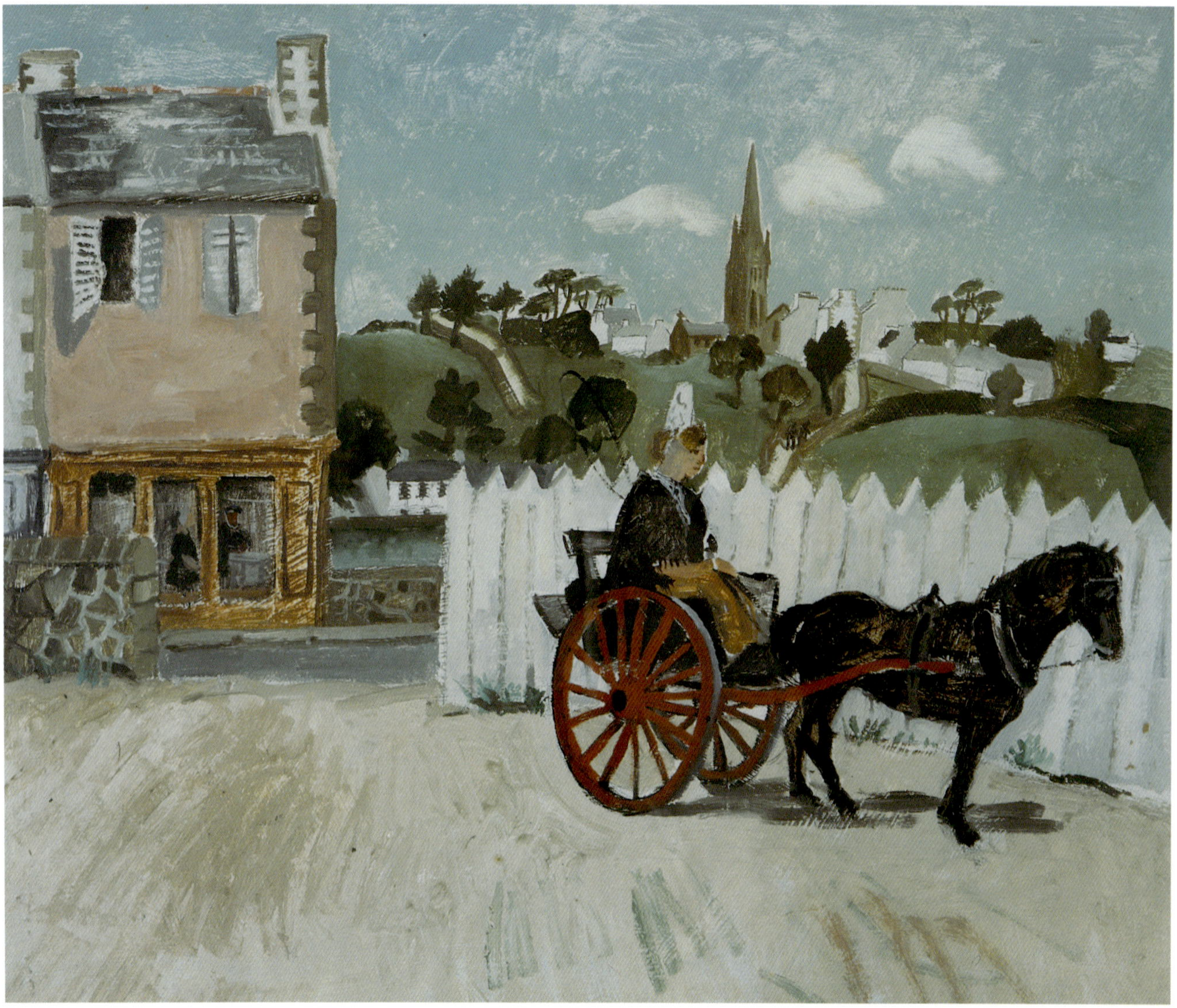

17 **Pony and Trap, Ploaré, Brittany**
1930

Oil on canvas 52.5 × 64 cm
The Dartington Hall Trust

The scene shows an enclosed courtyard facing onto the avenue de la Gare, Tréboul, site of the railway station that served both Tréboul and Douarnenez. From here, the avenue led in one direction to the harbour and into the town of Tréboul: in the other direction it led to the bridge across the Port Rhu and thence to Douarnenez, a route with which Christopher Wood was probably familiar. The subject matter is emphatically ordinary, a familiar scene on the busy Tréboul–Douarnenez road (the village of Ploaré referred to in the title is on the outskirts of Tréboul). A horse and cart is standing in what is perhaps the station forecourt, and the woman holding the reins may simply be waiting to meet someone from the train. She wears traditional peasant costume, with the *borléden* headdress of the Quimper region.

The 'pony' of the title refers to what appears to be a disproportionately small horse in relation to the woman and the cart. In the Breton countryside at this time, ponies were in fact never used for drawing such vehicles, but Wood invariably refers to the horses in his paintings as ponies.

Wood creates contrasts both between the left and right sides of the composition, and between the different vertical planes from the space of the courtyard to the tall steeple of Ploaré that dominates the surrounding countryside. In the lower centre can be seen the waters of the Port Rhu and a house on the quayside. Wood has intentionally distorted the spatial relationship between the various planes of the composition, exploiting the different heights of the houses and making the steeple even taller, while creating his own version of the relationship between the two sides of the valley.

A quick glance at this painting leaves the impression of a naive, picturesque simplicity. But by giving no indication as to why the woman is waiting, Wood allows a sense of mystery to linger, inviting the viewer to imagine a narrative.

AC

18 **Tréboul** 1930

Oil on canvas 53.3 × 72.4 cm
Private Collection

This painting shows small sailing boats on a slipway set beside an unidentified seaside church, with a view of houses on a distant headland. Wood's return to Brittany in the early summer of 1930 was partly in search of the solitude that he had discovered there the previous year, and also to escape from his hectic social life in Paris. In a postcard from Dieppe to Ben Nicholson in 1929, he wrote 'F[roska] and I are here and are very pleased. It's a bit like B'shead as far as the temperature is concerned but lacks the nice quiet places and wild distances. Otherwise it is just what I like, not too much of anything, lovely houses, port, cliffs with green grass and the kind of boats that Mr Wallis used to sail in' (TGA 8618).

The abandoned boats on the slipway emphasise a lack of human presence, and the air of mystery of the painting is augmented by a glimpse of sails of a boat, otherwise hidden by the church. The coexistence of religious belief and everyday life, which Wood so admired in the Breton people, is explicit in this work, with the two elements presented either side of the starkly painted wall running down the edge of the slipway.

MR

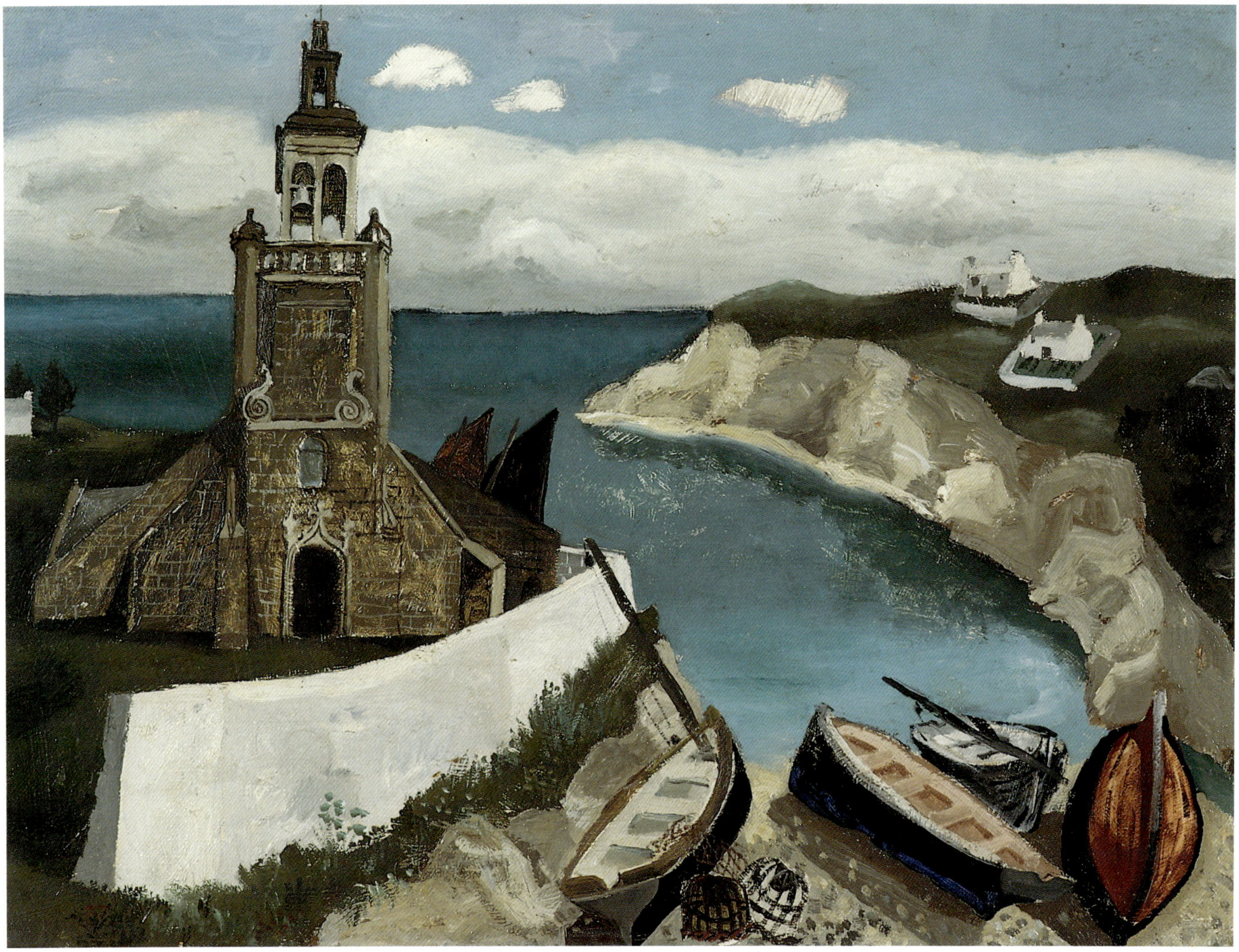

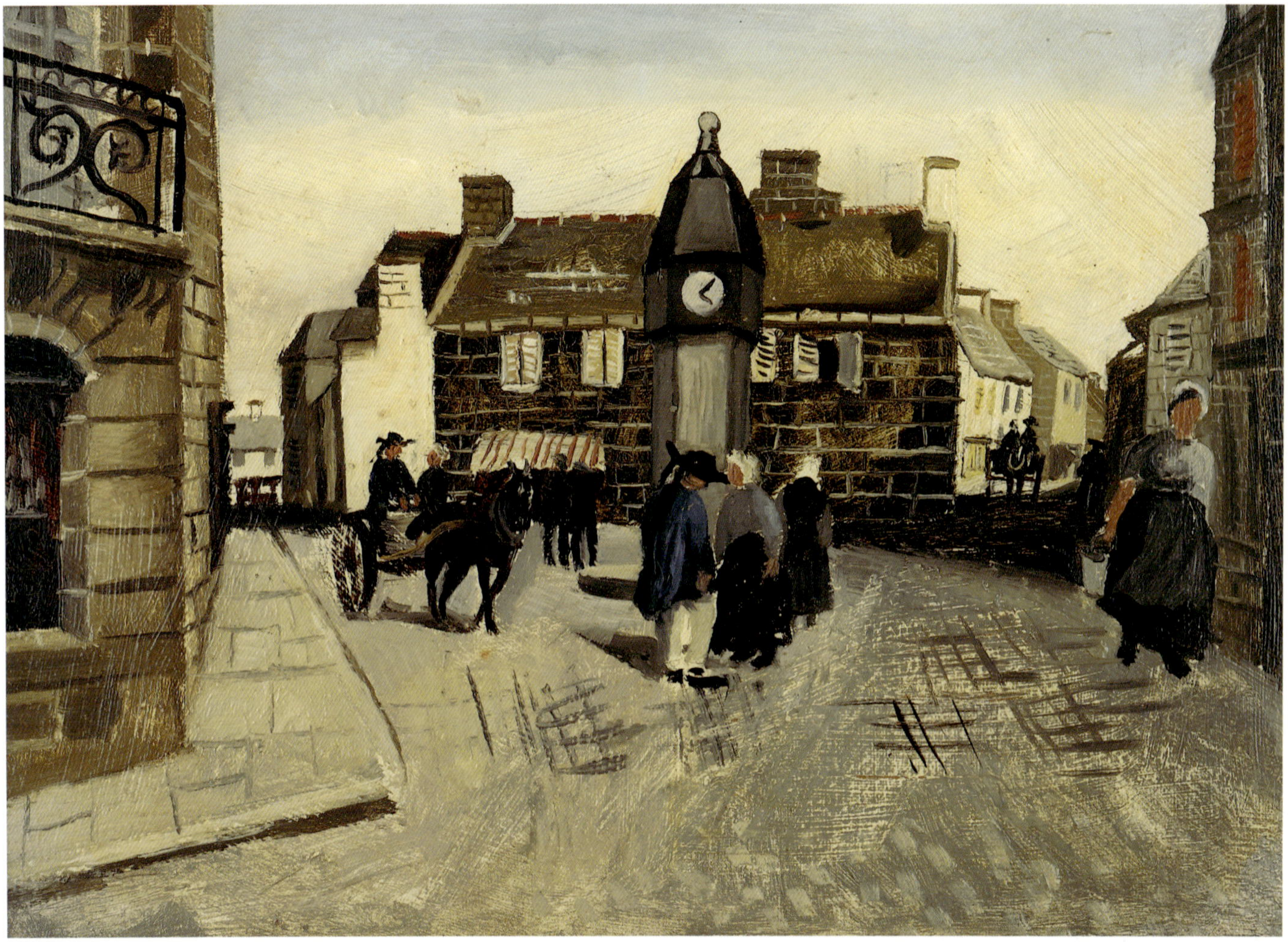

19 **Douarnenez, Brittany** 1930

Oil on board 33 × 45.7 cm
Tate Gallery, London. Bequeathed by Alberta, Duchess of Sandwich

Weary of painting boats and ports, as he explained in a letter of 1930 to the Nicholsons, Wood decided to concentrate more on architectural subjects, the stable, solid qualities of which prompted him to create 'more peaceful compositions'. His series of works showing churches and chapel interiors from Tréboul dates from this time, as well as scenes such as this one of the streets and squares of Tréboul and Douarnenez.

This painting depicts the place de la Croix (now place Gabriel Peri), the historic centre of Douarnenez's working-class district. Wood shows the square on a bright sunny afternoon, as indicated by the time shown on the face of the town clock (which has since been removed). The square's general layout has changed very little since Wood painted this picture; it is still defined by the rue Sainte-Hélène to the left, which leads from Les Halles (the market) to the port, and to the right to the Grand'Rue (now rue Anatole France).

The topographic accuracy of Wood's rendering of this scene reveals his use of postcard views. There are particularly striking similarities with a postcard in the Villard collection, where one can see the large house just behind the clock and the apartment blocks with their wrought-iron balconies on either side of the square (fig.25 on p.24). The only features missing in the painting are a public fountain surmounted by an Egyptian statuette, behind the town clock (which is shown in a simplified form with one face instead of three and unadorned with advertisements), the sign of a shoe shop to the right, and a group posing for the photographer at the base of the clock – no doubt too stiff and formal to be included in the painting.

The liberties Wood has taken with his photographic source are combined with qualities in his free handling of the paint, for example the play of colour contrasts between the dark brushmarks of the figures and the luminous ochres of the buildings, or the almost tactile translation of the cobbled surface of the square and the stones of the houses into roughly textured paint, scratched in places to reveal the board beneath.

As in numerous other paintings, Wood is engaged here in showing the daily routine of ordinary people, wearing their traditional dress, such as the peasant couple who have come to town in their cart or the couple gossiping in the middle of the square. The only dissonant note in this calmly balanced composition is struck by the female figure to the right, with her strange proportions and accelerated movement.

SB

20 **Breton Woman at Prayer** 1930

Oil on board 53.3 × 64.7 cm
Southampton City Art Gallery

After Wood's death, Max Jacob wrote 'I have seen the pious and honest girls who served us wiping away tears and I am sure that they have prayed for his soul.' This woman could be one of those girls, caught unawares kneeling in the chapel of Saint-Jean, near the Hôtel Ty-Mad in Tréboul. Wood loved the chapel's blue ceiling, naive statues and whitewashed walls. In his work he is often the wistful observer of the figures' sense of rootedness; they appear to be uncomplicated but he manages to express their very soul. Here the woman at prayer is perfectly integrated into the bare framework of the chapel (the dimensions of which have been reduced), which is treated in austerely muted colour.

FS-C

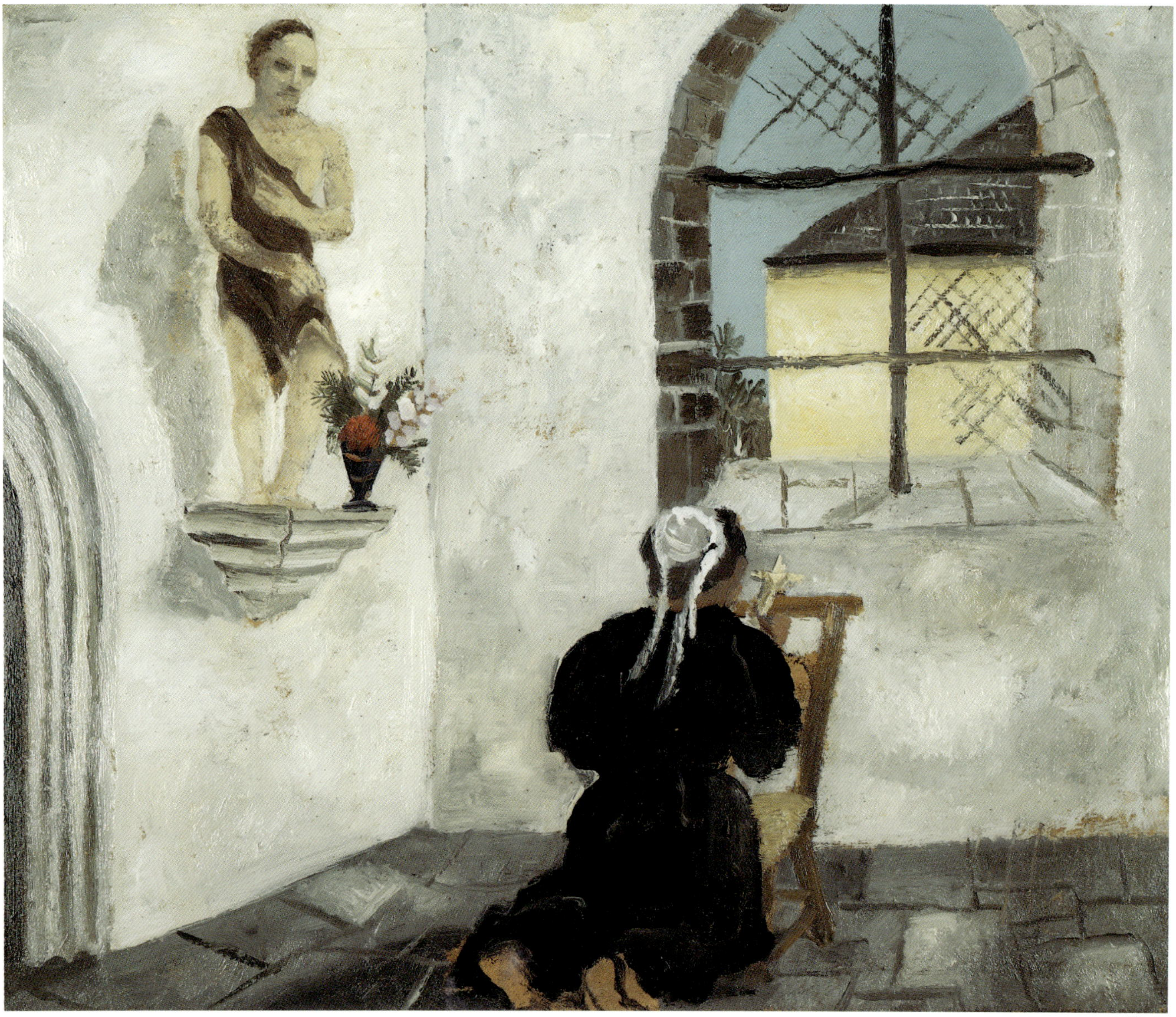

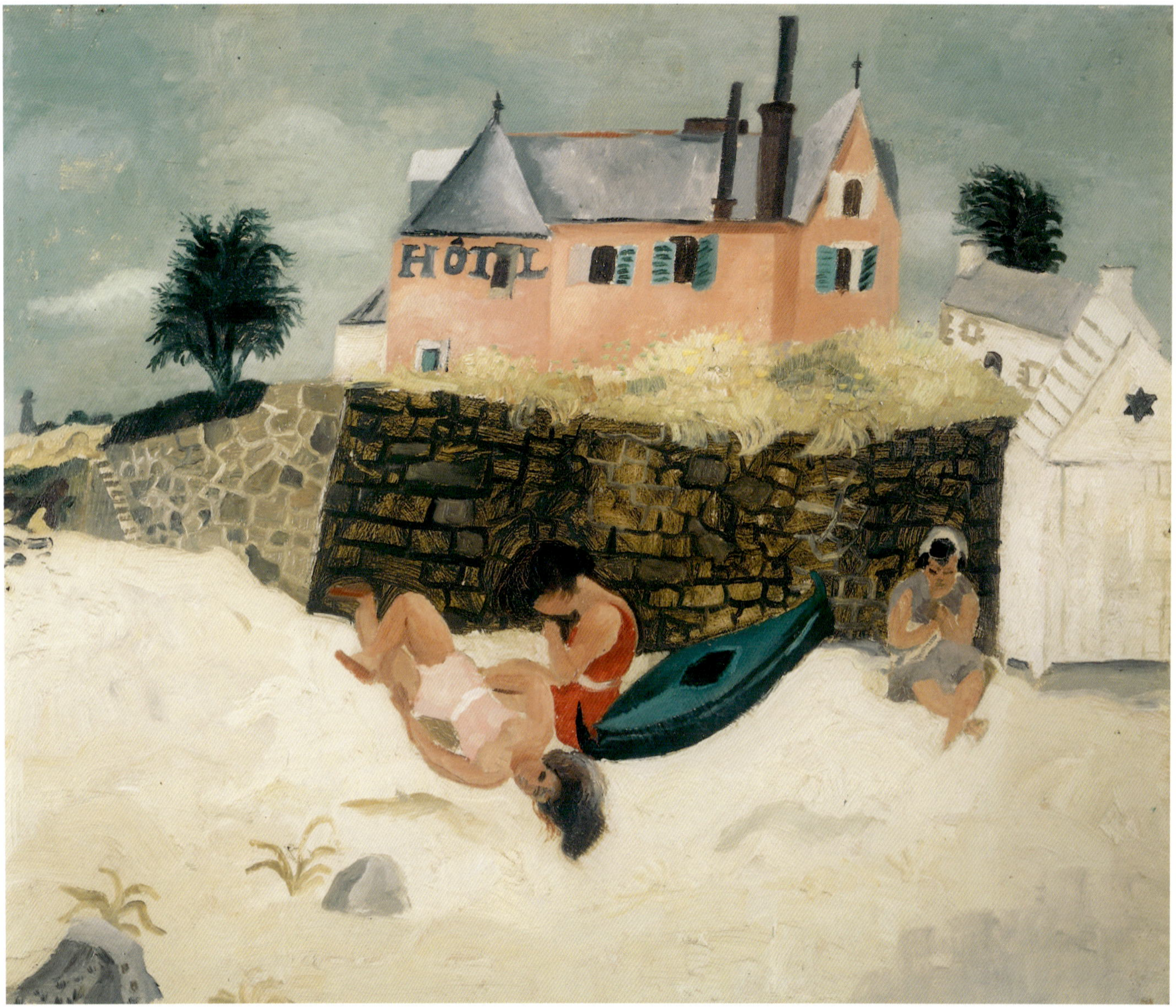

21 **The Plage, Hotel Ty-mad, Tréboul**
1930

Oil on canvas 45.7 × 54.6 cm
Sheffield City Art Galleries
[Not exhibited]

This painting dates from Wood's second stay in Tréboul, during the summer of 1930 when he and Max Jacob were staying at the Hôtel Ty-Mad. Wood's executor Rex Nan Kivell erroneously identified the Ty-Mad as the subject of this painting, which in fact shows the Hôtel des Sables Blancs (recently demolished) on the beach of the same name.

Wood's second visit to Brittany marked a decisive evolution in his style. His more intense palette can be linked to his increasing opium addiction. A luminous intensity, evoking a hallucinatory sense of well-being, is countered here by shadows and the use of black. The serenity of this beach scene infused with sunlight is only superficial: the motionless, self-contained poses of the three women create a sense of unease, reinforced by the gloomy bulk of the wall at the centre of the composition, and by the black used on the small green canoe and the beach hut.

As in almost all his paintings, Wood mixes aspects of observed reality with imaginative elements. Thus the stone wall, the little house of grey granite and the beach hut reflect physical reality, while the pink tone of the hotel facade, which echoes the colour of the bathing costume worn by the woman lying on the sand, expresses less tangible artistic preoccupations, glimpsed in Wood's strange question quoted by Max Jacob: 'Why don't Breton people like pink?'

The balance of the composition is disturbed by the contorted figure of the woman in pink, reminiscent of the distorted bodies of Picasso's female bathers, seen by Wood seven years earlier.

The modernity of this apparently simple and naive painting was noted by Augustus John at the time of the Redfern Gallery exhibition in London in 1938.

SB

22 **Anemones in a Cornish Window**
1930

Oil on canvas 40.6 × 50.8 cm
Leeds Museums and Galleries (City Art Gallery)

The imagery of this work makes it the clearest representation of Wood's affinities with the work of Winifred Nicholson: the motif of the pot plant or vase of flowers on window ledge appears in her paintings as early as 1922. Wood had made paintings of such motifs while working alongside Winifred during his stay at Banks Head in the spring of 1928.

The dating of this work derives from the list in Eric Newton's catalogue. Such a date would suggest that it was perhaps painted in Mousehole, the only possible location of a 'Cornish Window' in Wood's travels that year. However, the view does not appear to be of Mousehole. The work's composition suggests the amalgamation of two distinct spaces, the foreground still life and the background harbour view. The harbour view may suggest details of the St Ives townscape – the shape of the Mariners' Church, the Sloop Inn, the Island above and behind – yet the hills to the left recall the Cumberland landscapes of 1928. Furthermore, the light, fresh hues and dense, direct application of paint relate the picture more to work of the previous two years.

The uncertainly over the subjects of this and other works not only reflects the imprecise nature of the lists made in 1938 by Eric Newton and Rex Nan Kivell, but also stems from Wood's working methods. Working in temporary studios as he travelled, he would often complete works from sketches, photographs and from memory, away from the scene that may originally have stirred his imagination.

MT

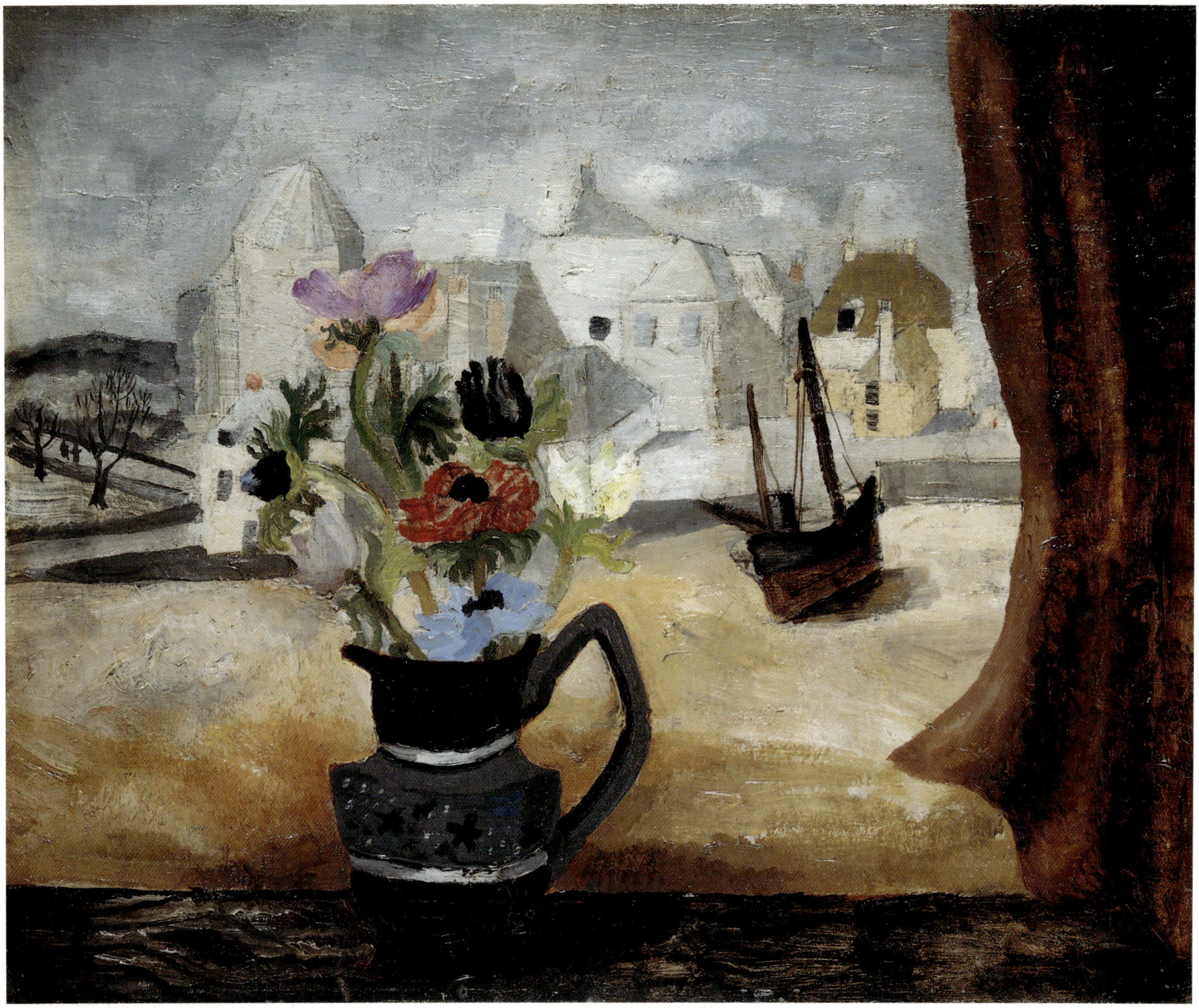

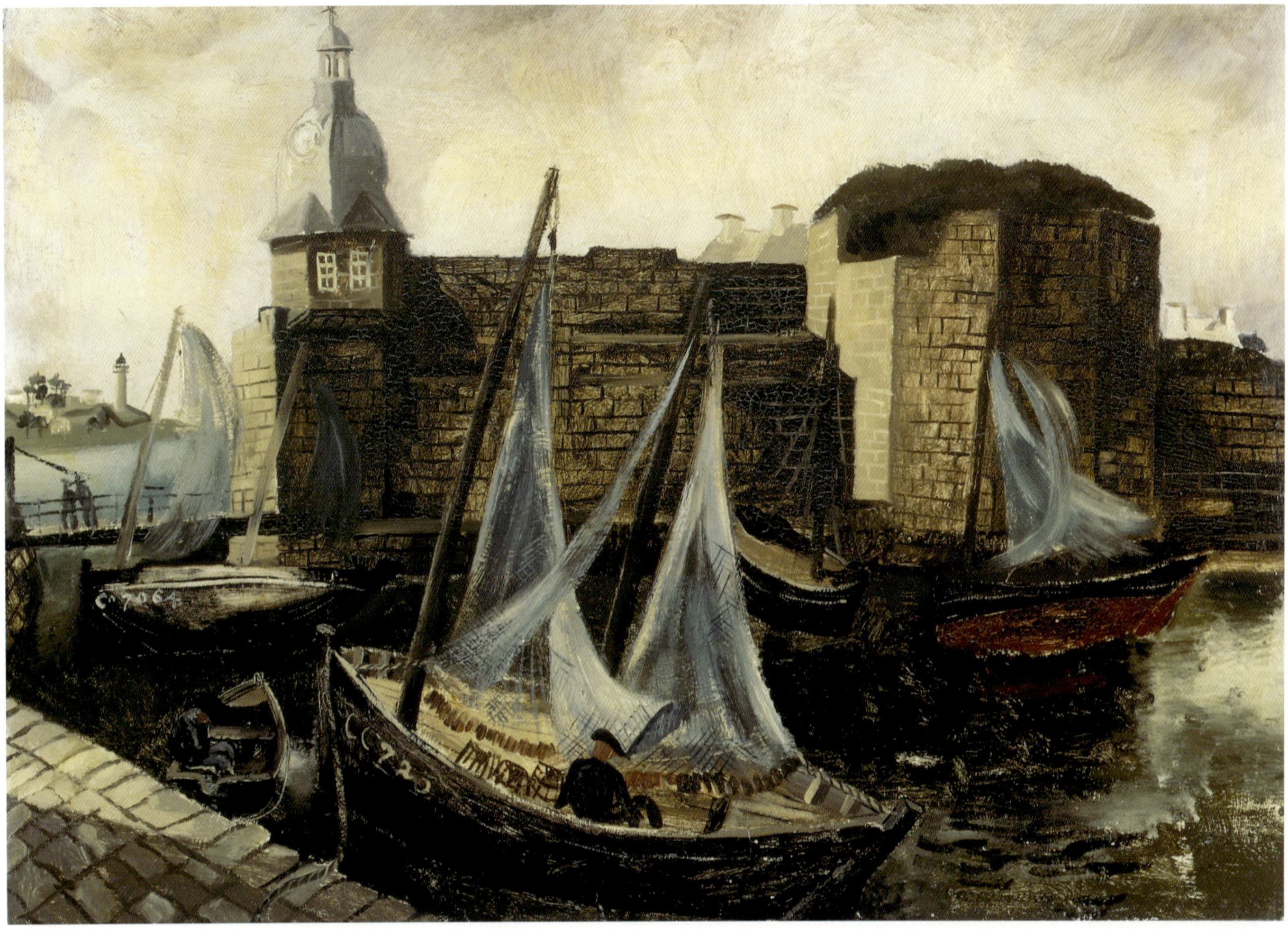

23 **La Ville Close, Concarneau, Brittany** 1930

Oil on board 57.2 × 81.2 cm
The Syndics of the Fitzwilliam Museum, Cambridge

Wood would probably have heard about the port of Concarneau, which was a popular location for artists, during his first visit to Brittany in 1929.

The absence, however, of any reference in Wood's copious correspondence to a trip to Concarneau, together with the rarity of images of this port, make it likely that he based this painting on a postcard. The accuracy of his rendering of both the medieval ramparts and the belfry housing the sundial clock tends to support this interpretation.

A regular visitor to seaports, from St Ives to Tréboul, Marseilles and Dieppe, Wood never tired of repeating the motif of the fishing boat with wind-filled sails, ready to tackle the ocean. The moment he has chosen to represent in this work, however, is one of waiting and repose, symbolised by the two idle fishermen.

Wood's restricted palette here, limited to the blues of the sails, the luminous ochres of the sun-drenched ramparts, and the browns of the boats' hulls, contributes to a sense of poetic realism, reinforcing the feeling of serenity or 'dreamlike peace' that he believed he had found in Brittany.

SB

24 **Street in Tréboul** 1930

Oil on board 55.2 × 66 cm
Lloyds TSB Group plc

This work is often referred to as one of the most obvious examples of Wood's use of a postcard as a source. Nevertheless, there are a number of differences between this image and the original postcard (fig.26 on p.24). As well as the general layout and obvious architectural details, Wood preserves the rake of the shadow on the wall and the woman in traditional costume at the left, but he eliminates from the centre of the composition all the other figures that appear in the postcard. This creates a distinct emptiness in the heart of the work, with the street ahead now deserted. The church spire is shifted slightly to the right so as to appear as the furthest point at the end of the street.

MT

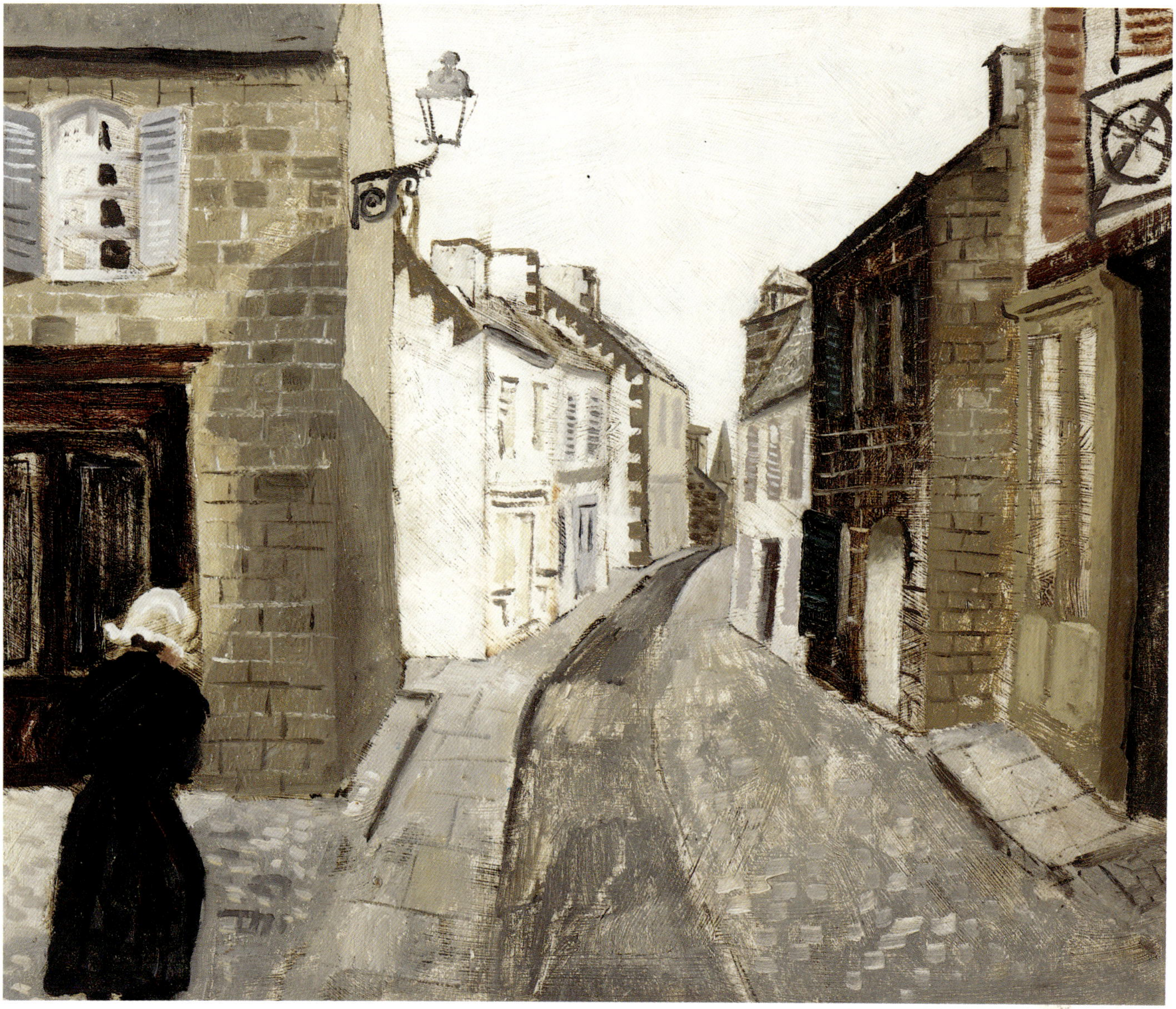

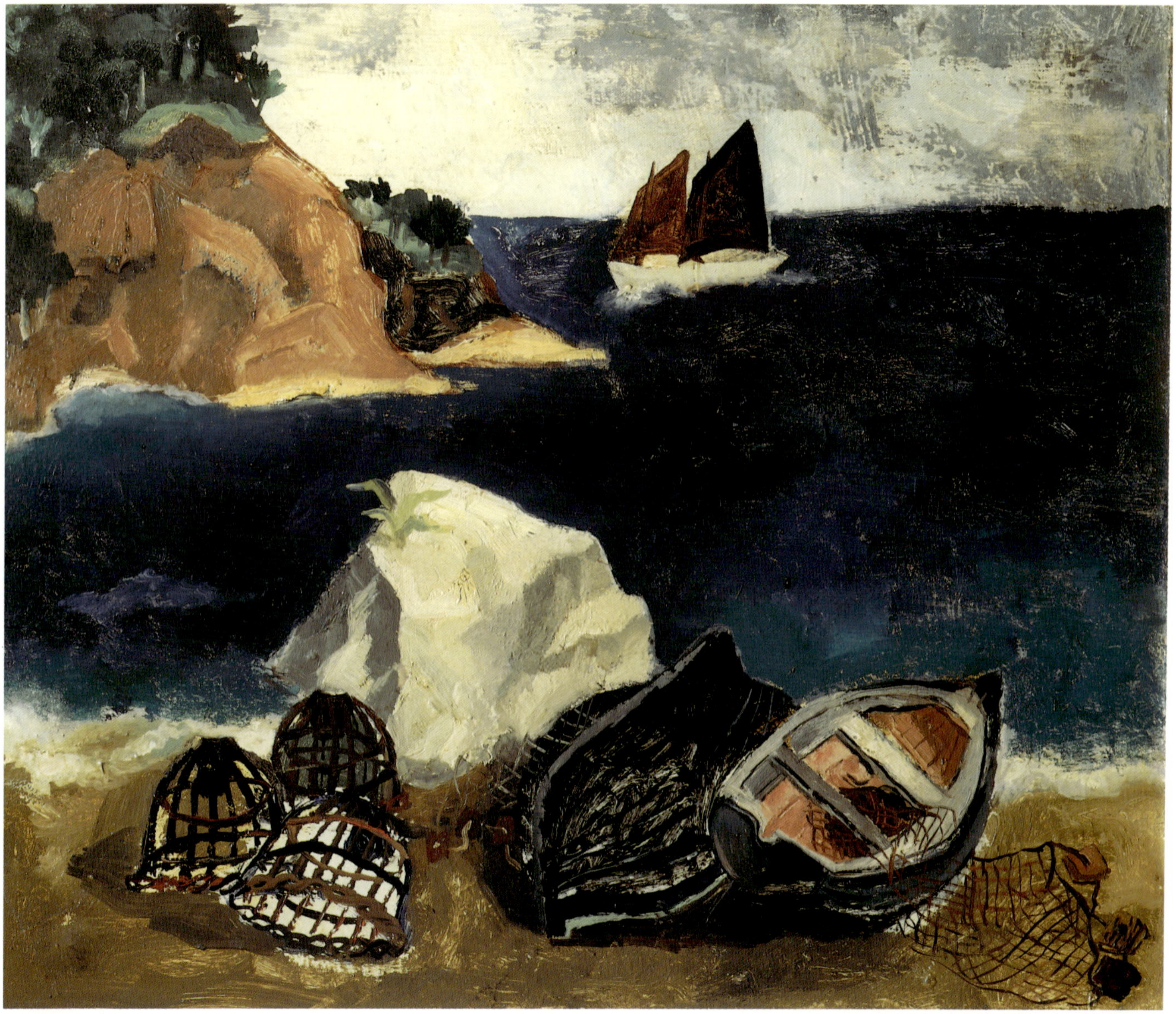

25 **Tréboul 1930** 1930

Oil on canvas 45.7 × 54.6 cm
Private Collection

Like *Le Phare* (no.14) this work (now generally known as *Tréboul, the Blue Sea*) evokes Alfred Wallis in its simple depiction of the Breton coastline. The composition includes a subtle counterpoint in the foreground: upturned boat alongside upright boat, nets opposed to lobster pots, all grouped around a rock. Wood was preoccupied with the fishing boat as an image of the fragility of life. This was an idea he expressed on grander scale in his subjects of boats under construction or in harbour (see nos.37, 38), and this painting can be seen as a quiet elegy echoing the sentiments of such works.

MT

26 **Sleeping Fisherman, Ploaré, Brittany** 1930

Oil on canvas 37.8 × 72.8 cm
Laing Art Gallery, Newcastle upon Tyne

Wood derived the elements in the background of this painting from a postcard that he annotated (fig.28 on p.24) of the beach of Saint-Jean at Tréboul – not Ploaré, as the title would suggest. He leaves out some details but introduces the powerful figure of the sleeping youth, who is more akin to a mythical deity than a Breton fisherman. The mystery of this presence, the strange imbalance in proportions, the two contrasting techniques in which paint is thickly applied in the landscape setting whilst the figure is delicately drawn, and the turbulence of the sky and sea against the stillness of the body combine to imbue this canvas with a poetic realism of its own.

FS-C

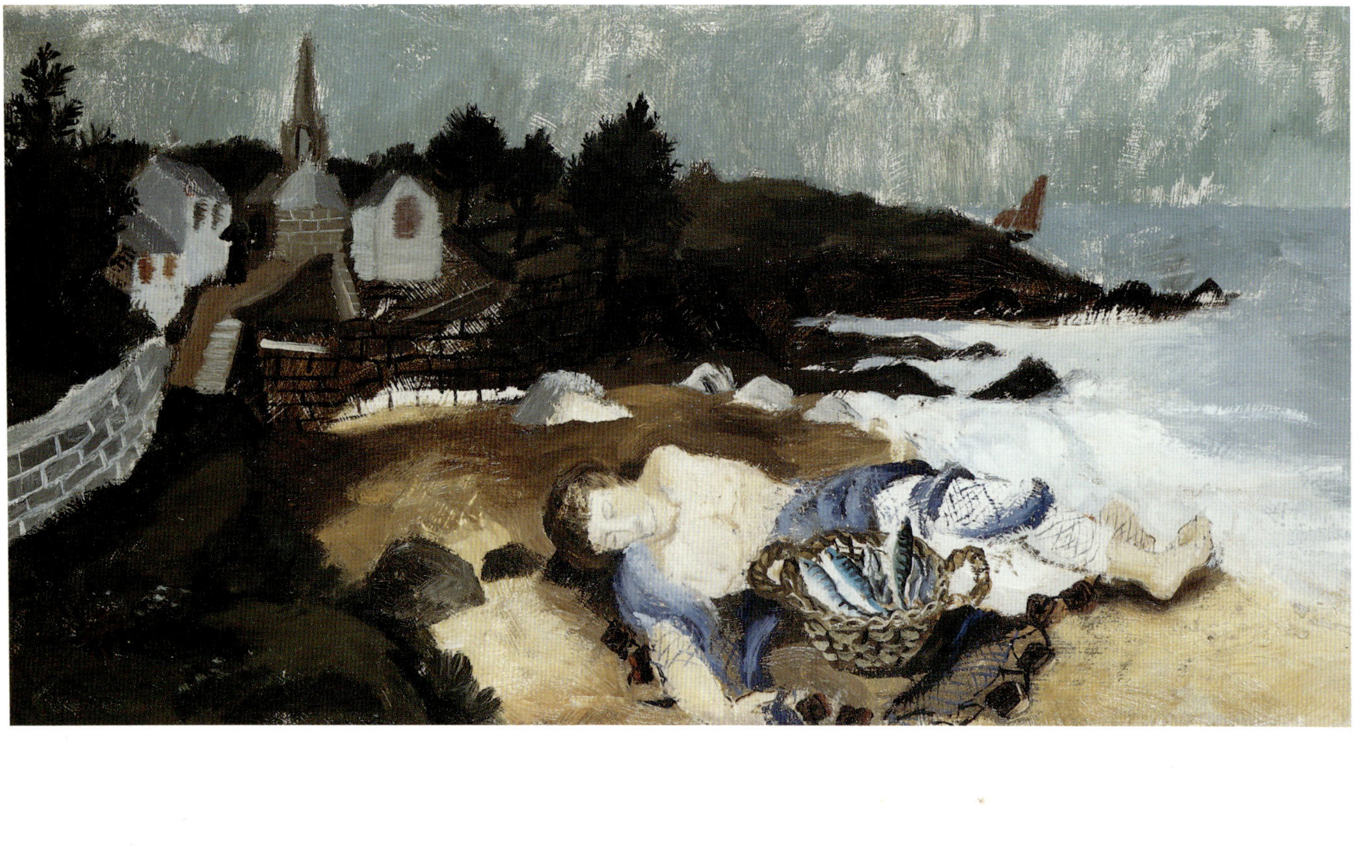

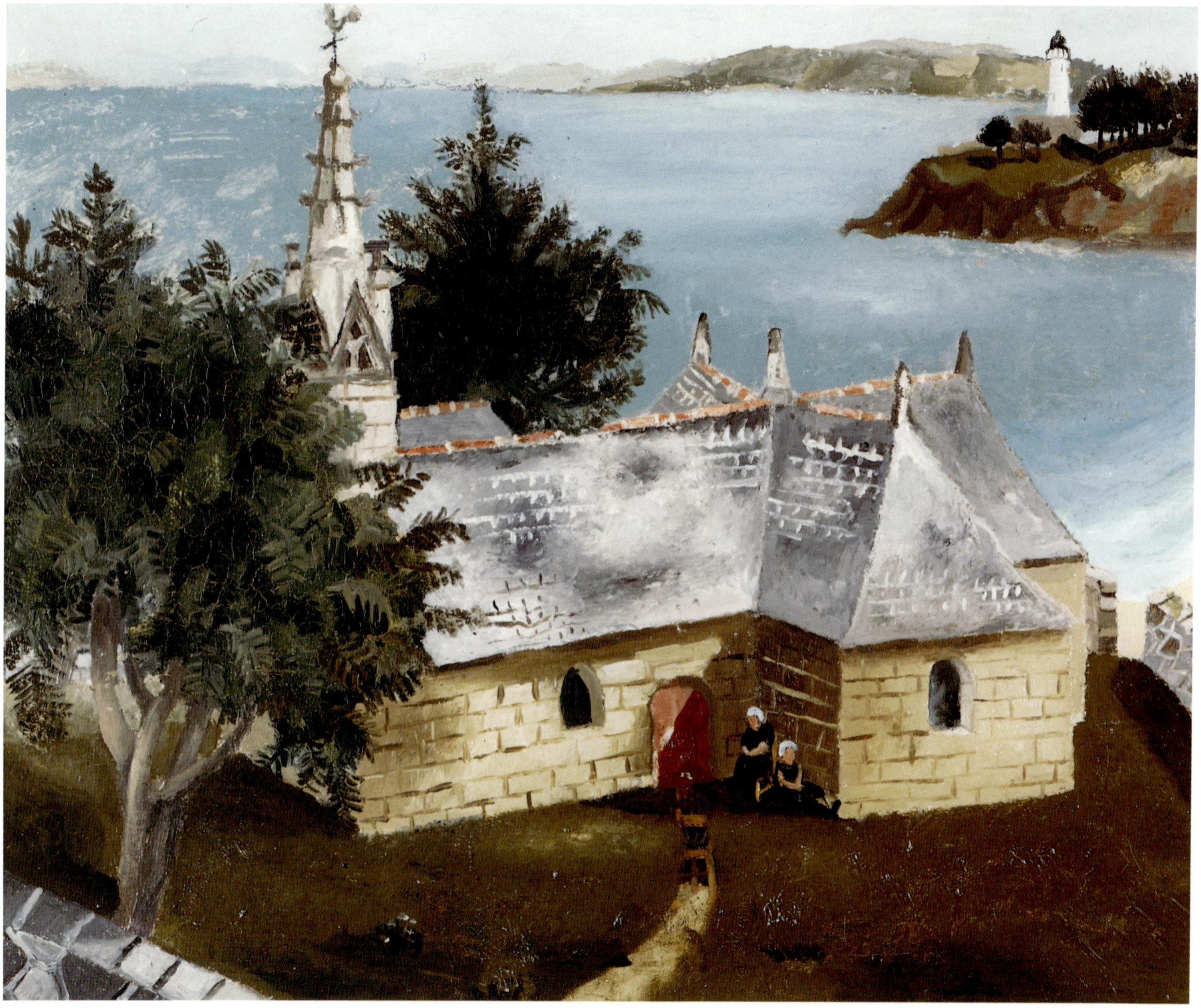

27 **La Trémouille Church, Tréboul**
1930

Oil on canvas 61 × 76.2 cm
Private Collection

Unusually, this view is not elaborated with additional details or imagined transpositions. It is a straightforward depiction of the view from the window of Wood's room at the Hôtel Ty-Mad in Tréboul, with slight changes in scale: Wood has enlarged the background view of the Île Tristan and its lighthouse surrounded by trees.

MT

28 **Dancing Sailors, Brittany** 1930

Oil on canvas 57.2 × 81.3 cm
Leicestershire Museums and Art Galleries

Winifred Nicholson described this canvas as 'the picture of pure joy – the only one he ever painted'. The colours are indeed bright and the scene is free of shadow. The sailors dancing beneath the bunting have frank, honest faces. Used to the freedom of the open sea, they are held here within the circle of cottages, their bodies locked into the rhythm of the dance. One of them drifts drunkenly away. Describing a similar scene, Wood commented (TGA 723): 'they are decent people and everything they do is done with a straightforward look. My life is so disordered' – a feeling that informs this canvas and its nostalgic effect.

FS-C

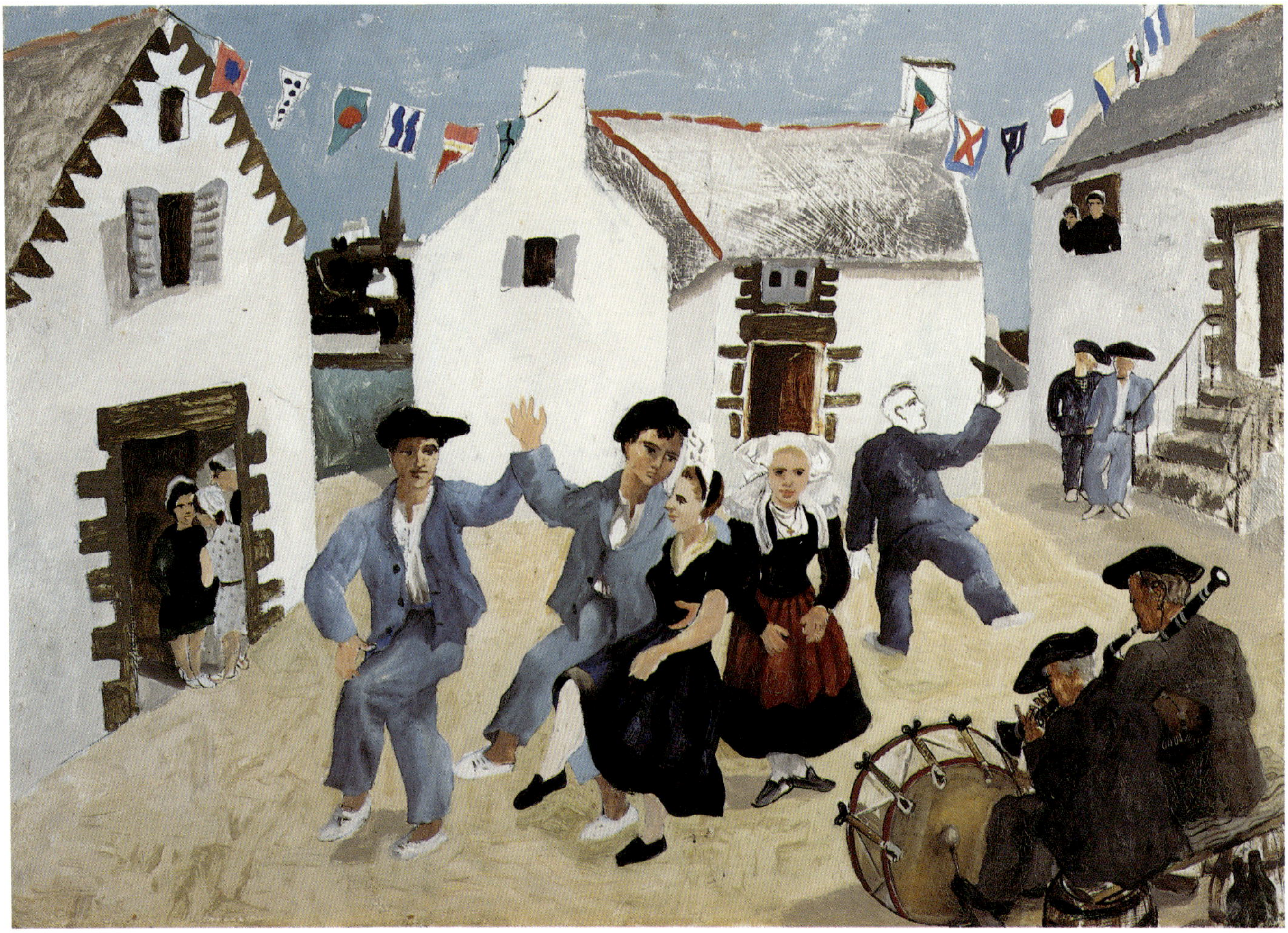

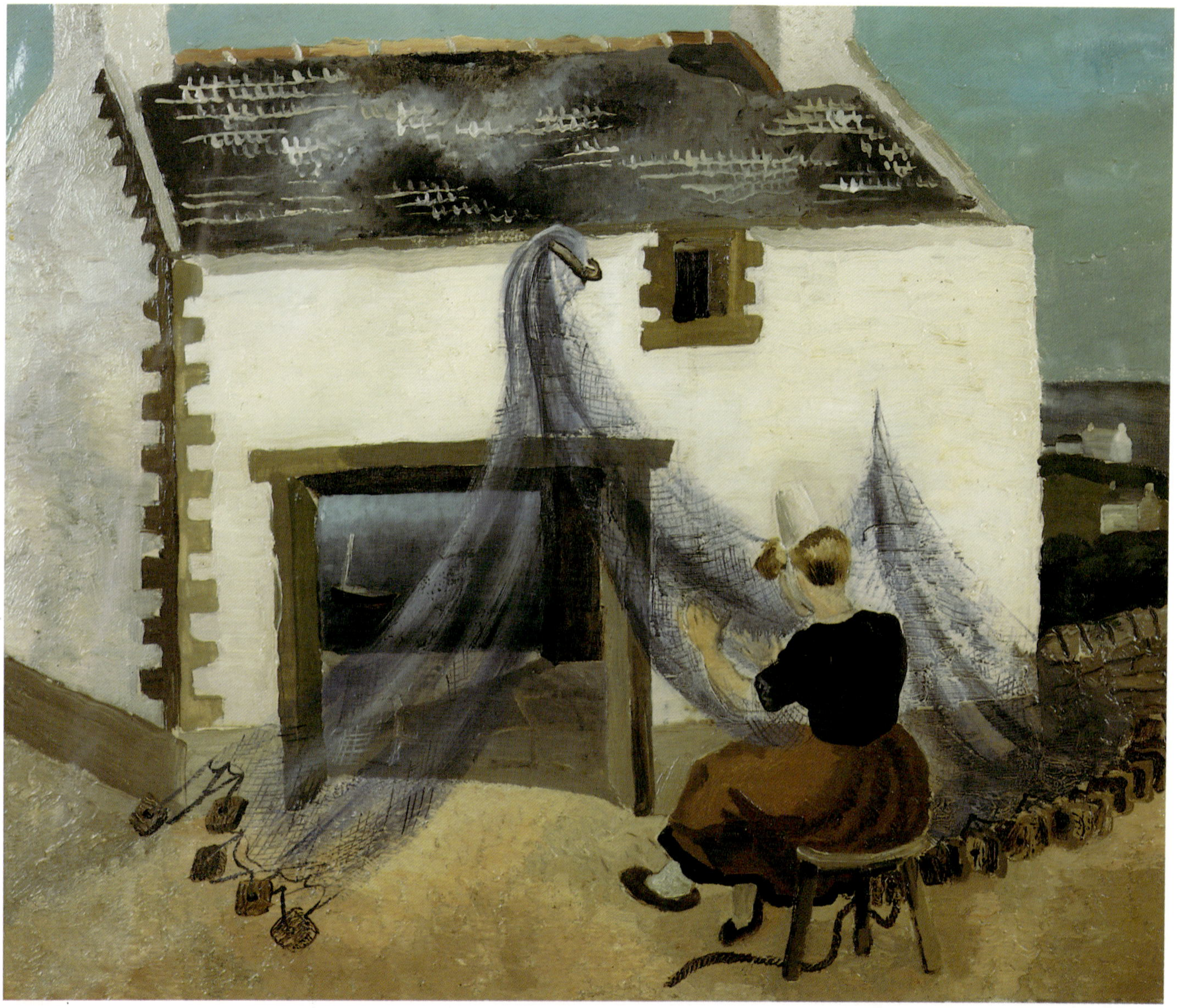

29 **Mending the Nets, Tréboul** 1930

Oil on canvas 78.7 × 109 cm
Private Collection

This work, which combines two of Wood's favourite subjects, local craft skills and the wearing of traditional dress, was painted by Wood in direct response to the daily life in Tréboul. The position of the town, on a promontory above the open sea, also prompted his imaginative use of the view through the harbour building to the sea beyond.

Winifred Nicholson saw *Mending the Nets* at Wood's last show, at the Galerie Georges Bernheim in Paris. She later wrote: 'His work in that exhibition was fine, dark and blocked. It was hard to see what his next move would be. One picture was different from anything else he had done. It was at Tréboul, of a woman mending nets against a white cottage. This was simple and mystic.' (Winifred Nicholson, 'Kit: A Memoire', manuscript, TGA 723)

MT

30 **Newlyn** 1930

Oil on canvas 52 × 62 cm
Glasgow Museums: Art Gallery and Museum, Kelvingrove

This work is now known as *The Harbour, Mousehole* but there is no mention of such a title in Eric Newton's list compiled in 1938. In the Redfern Gallery's photographic record of Newton's listing the painting is identified as *Newlyn* 1930 (EN 421).

Wood briefly stayed at Mousehole in March 1930, his only visit to Cornwall that year. He travelled there with his friend Peter Spencer, who left again almost immediately, leaving Wood on his own. Wood's return to Cornwall was occasioned by his need to assemble enough works for his forthcoming Paris exhibition, scheduled for early summer at Galerie Georges Bernheim. He wrote to his mother, in a letter dated 5 March 1930, 'I don't know how I can possibly do it, the only chance is to go quietly to a place I know and like and work all the time.' (TGA 773).

This painting has been retitled since 1938, partly because it bears little resemblance to the harbour at Newlyn, and also due to the inclusion of a small pillared house in the town background, which still stands today in Mousehole, albeit away from the quayside. However, the enclosed harbour scene is unlike even Mousehole and would appear to be an imagined view of a small rural harbour which combines memories of various places. The landscape in the background recalls the bare, textured landscapes that Wood had experienced and painted two years earlier while staying with the Nicholsons in Cumberland.

The painting illustrates Wood's interest in seeking connections between different geographical locations: as he wrote, in an excited letter to Ben Nicholson, inscribed 'Mousehole' and describing the town: 'behind these [Wood had described fishing boats at sea] is a hilly country almost like Bankshead [sic] and all the cliff is covered with daffodils and anemones. Lovely green fields, beige farms etc., its [sic] too wonderful' (TGA 8618).

MR

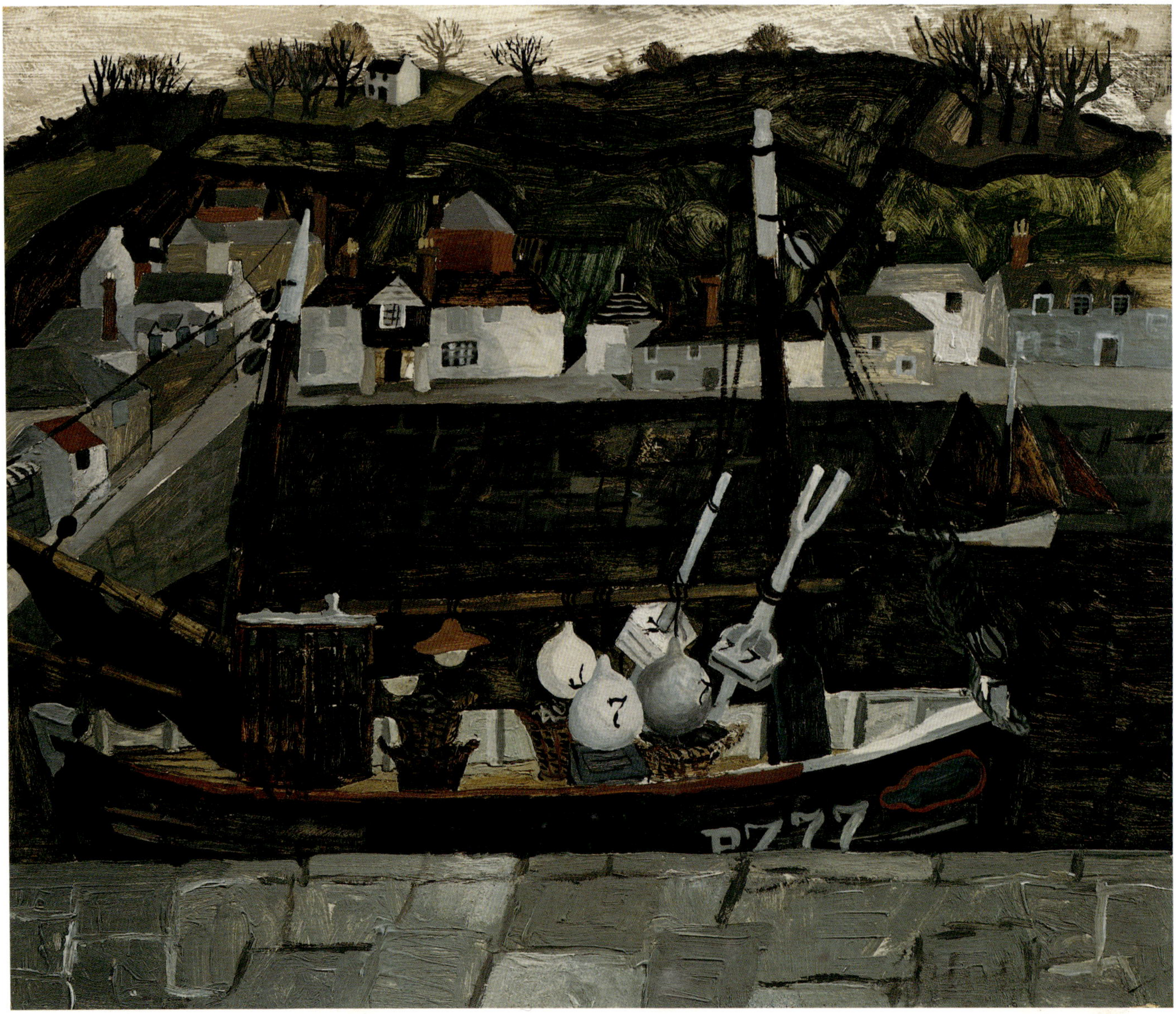

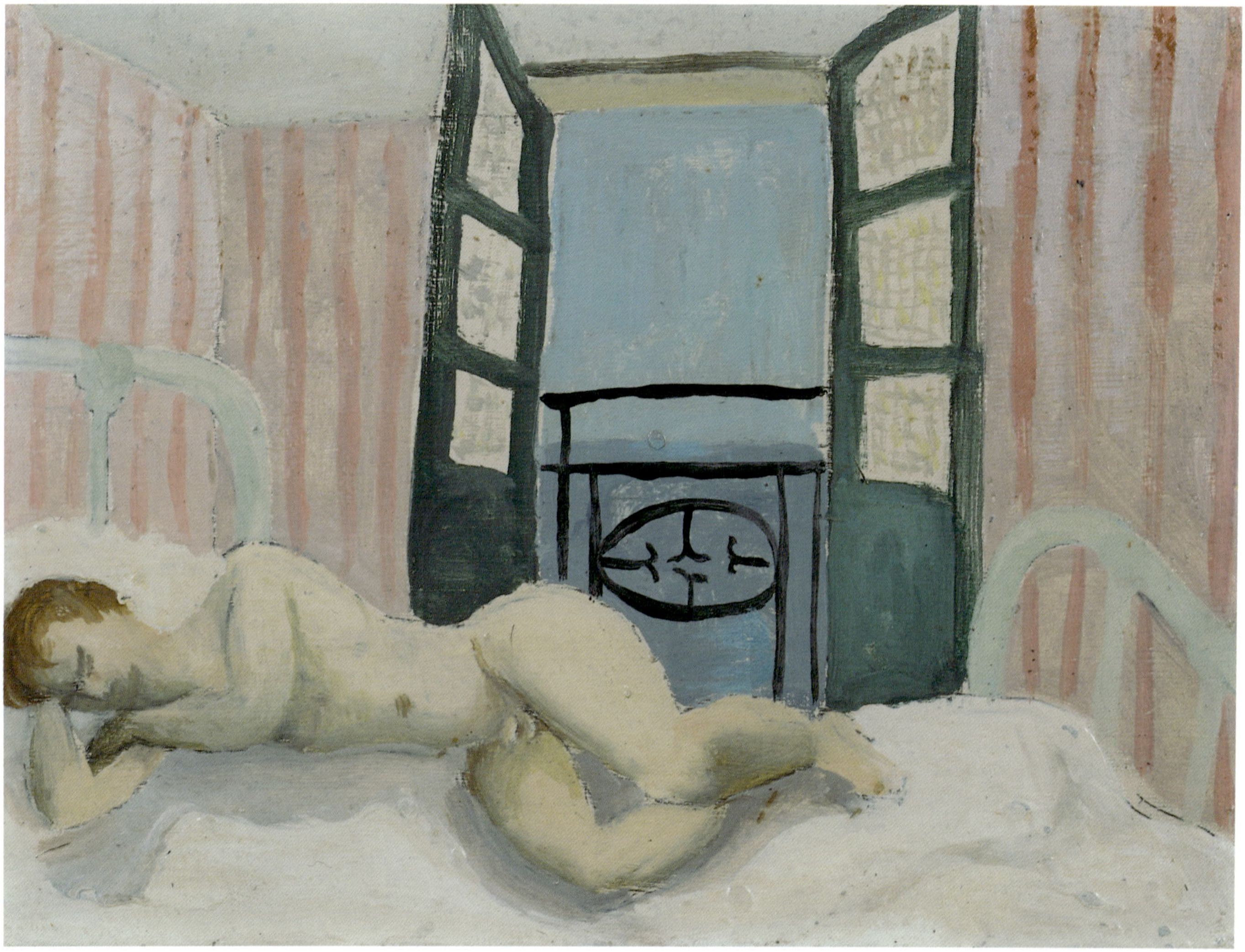

31 **Nude Boy in a Bedroom** 1930

Oil on panel 15.9 × 21 cm
Private Collection

This small painting is perhaps a preliminary study for the larger composition *Nude Boy in a Bedroom* (Scottish National Gallery of Art, Edinburgh; EN 391). It represents the interior of Wood's room at the Hôtel Ty-Mad, Tréboul, where he stayed for most of June and July 1930. The subject is said to be Francis Rose, a fellow artist and traveller who was also visiting Tréboul at this time.

There are a number of dissonances between this painting and the larger oil, not least the overall mood of the scene. Here the reclining figure seems to pose for the viewer; in the other work, which is a back view, the boy standing at the washbasin is glancing over his shoulder as if caught unawares. The decorative nature of the smaller work is emphasised by the colour scheme and the broad washes of paint, which also tend to flatten the scene.

There is a further small oil study of a similar subject (private collection; EN 424), which depicts the male figure standing and facing the viewer, which suggests a continuous narrative between the different moments represented in the three paintings.

MR

32 **Church at Tréboul** 1930

Oil on board 73 × 91.4 cm
Tate Gallery, London. Presented by Dr and Mrs Lucius Wood, the artist's parents

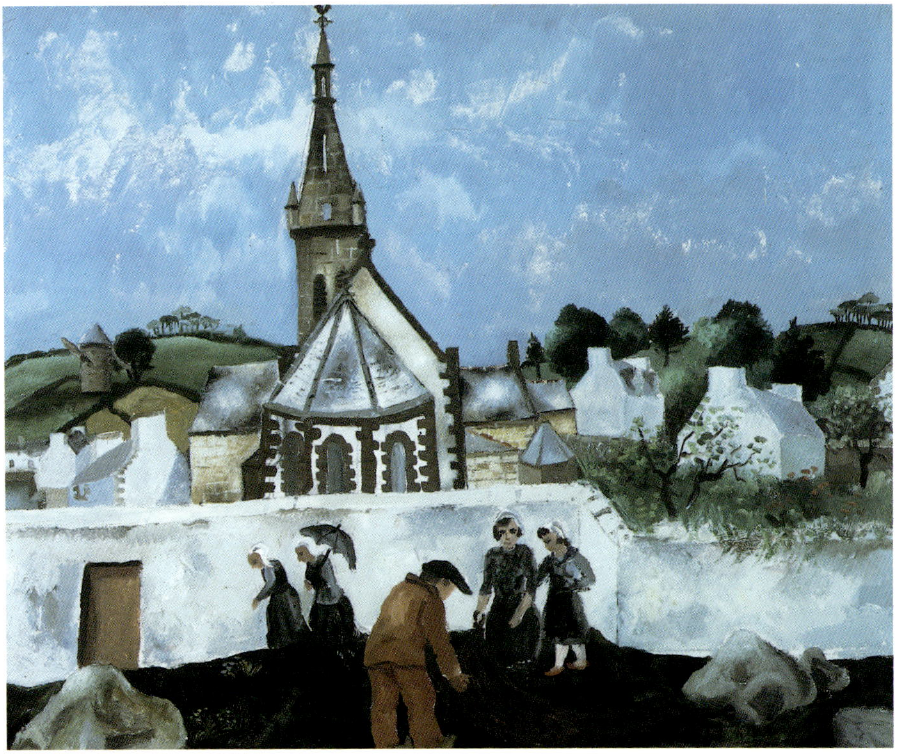

This view of the nineteenth-century church of Saint-Joseph in Tréboul was painted during Wood's last visit to Brittany, a time of great productivity for the artist. It shows the church from the east set within a rolling rural landscape. In the foreground, in front of a high wall, are a group of figures dressed in traditional costume. The viewpoint appears to be from one of the houses or gardens opposite, which today still partly overlook the church.

However, the church is actually set within the town of Tréboul and not on the outskirts as Wood has implied by including views out over a wooded landscape. The windmill to the left may be a symbol of the Breton countryside – just as Godrevy Lighthouse appears in many of Wood's paintings of St Ives irrespective of topographical location. A very similar windmill dominated a view of the Breton landscape painted by Cedric Morris in 1927, which Wood may well have seen.

The composition of foreground figures before a blank wall and the large bright sky tends to sandwich the view of the church, a sense exacerbated by the almost central thrust of the spire. The figures themselves lend the picture a certain symmetry, with pairs of women framing the figure of a bowed fisherman, and also suggest a narrative. The two pairs of woman are contrasted in age and in action, with the elder pair apparently hurrying through the scene intent on some purpose while the younger pair idly observe the labouring man.

MR

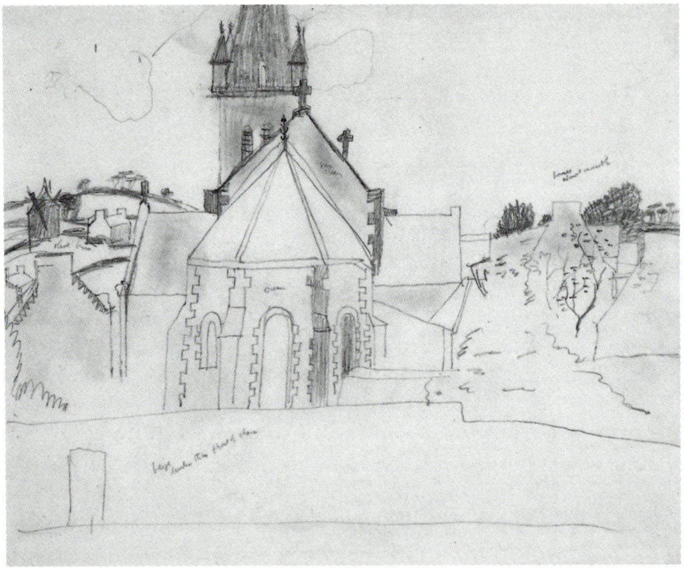

33 **Tréboul Church** 1930

Pencil on paper 30.5 × 37.8 cm
Tate Gallery, London

This drawing is the study for no.32. It is executed in pencil and includes the artist's colour annotations. It presents a slightly more focused view of the church from a similar angle, but cuts the spire and shows less of the surrounding landscape. The principal difference between the two works is that the empty foreground of the drawing has been filled with figures in the painting.

The colour notes, which range from 'olive brown', 'grey cream' to 'cream', suggest a more muted palette than was used for the painting. They possibly refer to a tinted black and white photograph or postcard that Wood may have used in his studio. However, the urgency and deliberateness of the line suggest that the drawing was executed quickly in front of the motif and later used in the studio for reference. The spareness of the image reveals Wood's increasing interest in the architectural design of his compositions.

MR

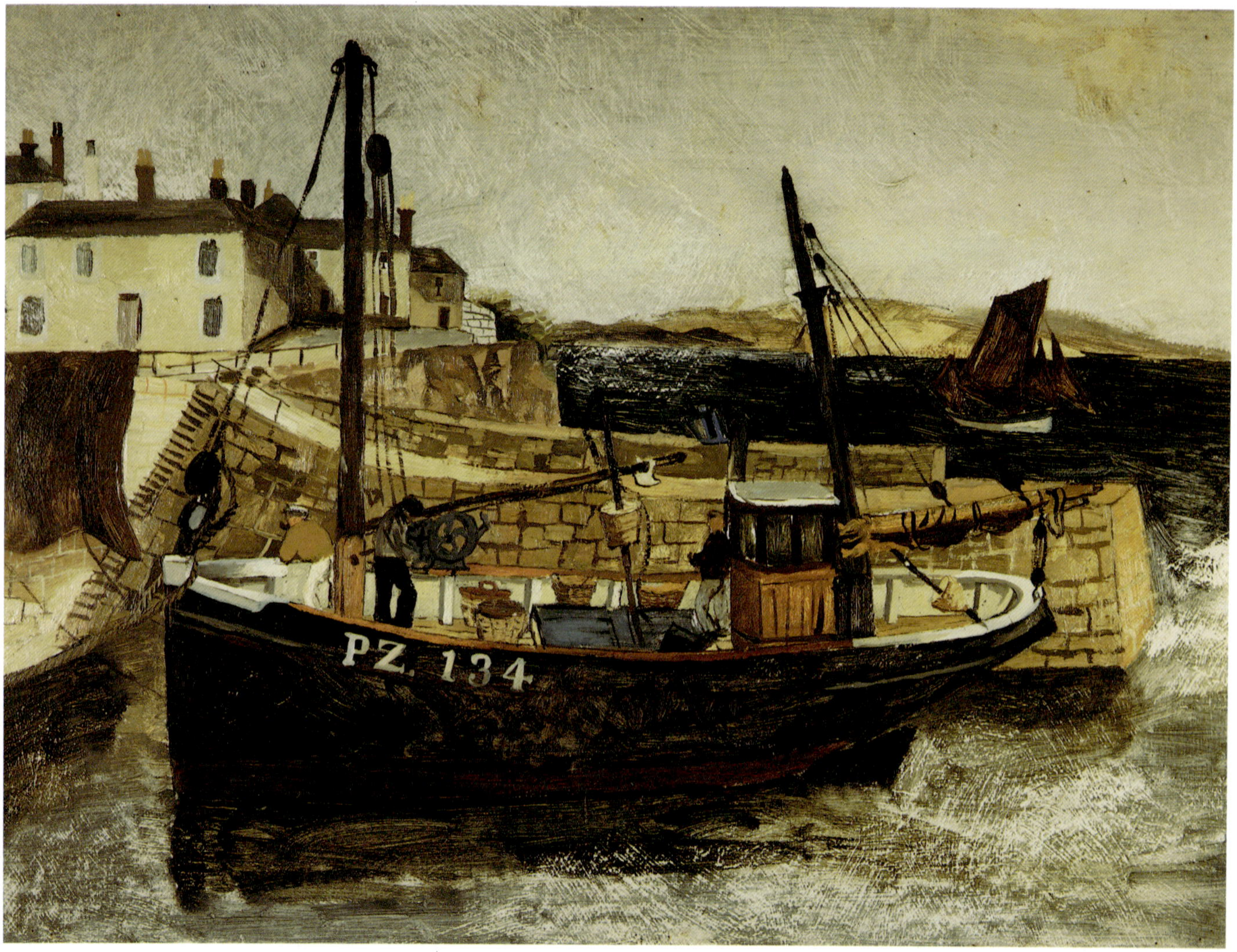

34 **P.Z. 134, Cornwall** 1930

Oil on board 50.8 × 71.1 cm
Towner Art Gallery and Museum, Eastbourne

The rooms that Wood rented during his brief stay in Mousehole in March 1930 looked directly out over the harbour and beyond into Mounts Bay. *P.Z. 134, Cornwall* takes this view as its backdrop. The subject of a boat in a harbour offers an interesting contrast to Wood's *Ship Leaving a Cornish Port*, painted in 1926 (no.3). As opposed to the fantastical quality of the earlier painting, *P.Z. 134, Cornwall* achieves an almost topographical accuracy in its depiction of a contemporary fishing vessel, complete with its correct Penzance registration marks, and shown contained within the high wall of Mousehole harbour.

The scarred surface of the painting is often ascribed to the example of Ben Nicholson's technique and is seen as an attempt to emphasise the painting's manufacture. It also reveals Wood's increasing confidence in his work and expresses a sense of urgency brought on both by his situation (he was preparing for his forthcoming exhibition and also attempting to give up opium) and by his return to his beloved Cornwall. Writing to Ben Nicholson, he explained: 'I won't write more as I am working at an enormous pace and absolutely deliriously happy painting. Never have I had such a delicious sensation from life before. I am quite alone as Peter Spencer went back the day after he arrived. It's wonderful to be able not to consider anything but ones want to work and to work and not to sleep and eat just when one wants' (TGA 8618).

MR

35 **Church at Tréboul** 1930

Oil on board 53.3 × 64.1 cm
Leeds Museums and Galleries (City Art Gallery)

This work shows a similar view to *Church at Tréboul* (no.33). However, there are a number of interesting differences between the two paintings. Again the church is seen as from the east, although it is now depicted from an oblique angle and from a slightly lower viewpoint. This perhaps suggests that it was painted from the garden of a house neighbouring the one that had offered the higher viewpoint in no.33. The open gateway in the foreground wall allows a view of the road, not apparent in the other painting. The angle and perspective of the church enables Wood to concentrate on it more closely and to eliminate most other details of its setting, no longer visible behind the wall.

Instead of the area in the foreground being a stage for human action, Wood paints two empty rowing boats – despite the church being inland from the sea. These suggest a human absence, perhaps alluding to the dangers of the sea or to the time spent by fishermen away from their families. In an evocative letter to Winifred Nicholson in 1929, Wood described the departure of the fishing fleet, commenting that 'The sailors' wives all dressed in black with white caps sat all together in a very small rowing boat and waited.' (TGA 8618).

MR

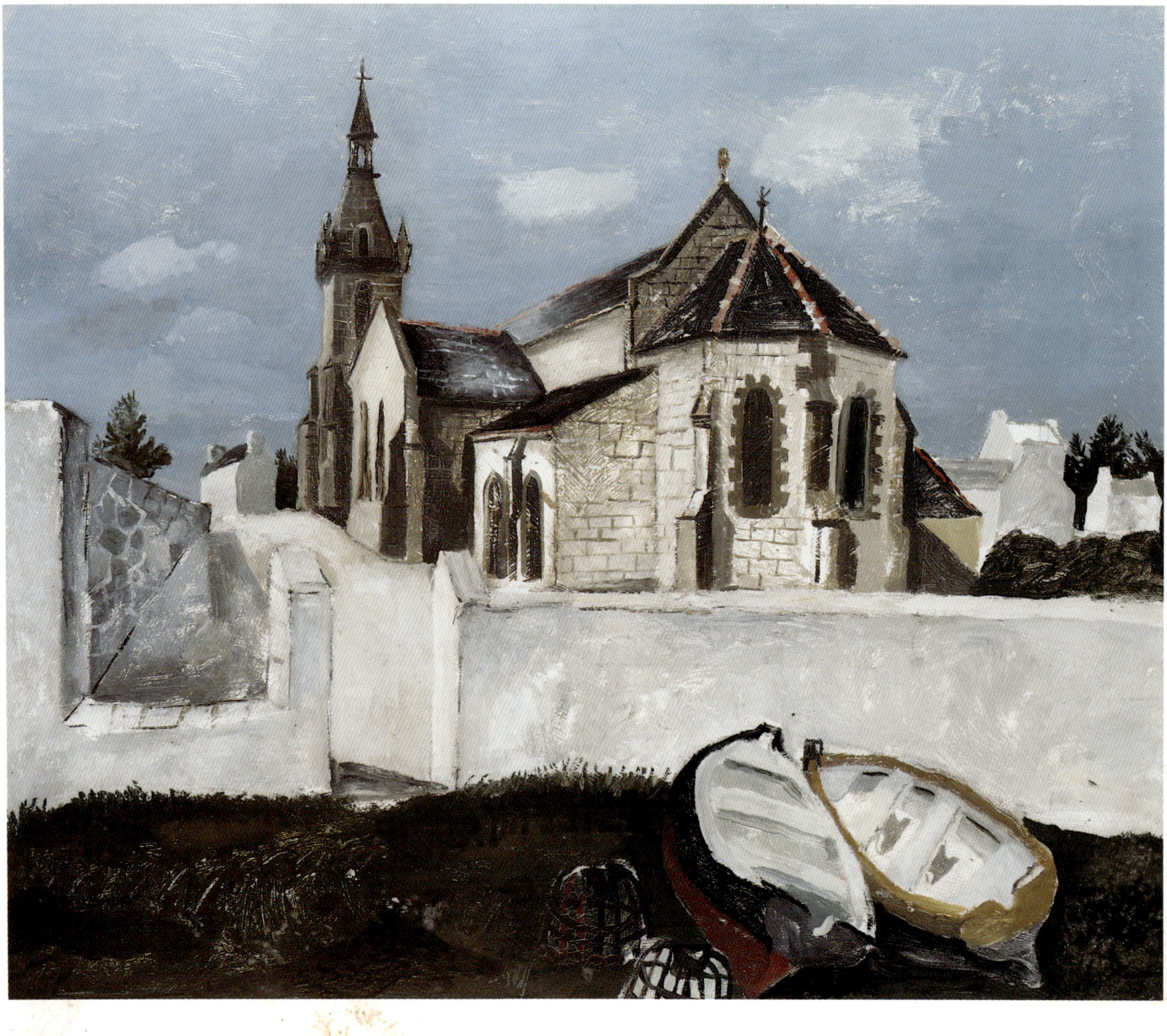

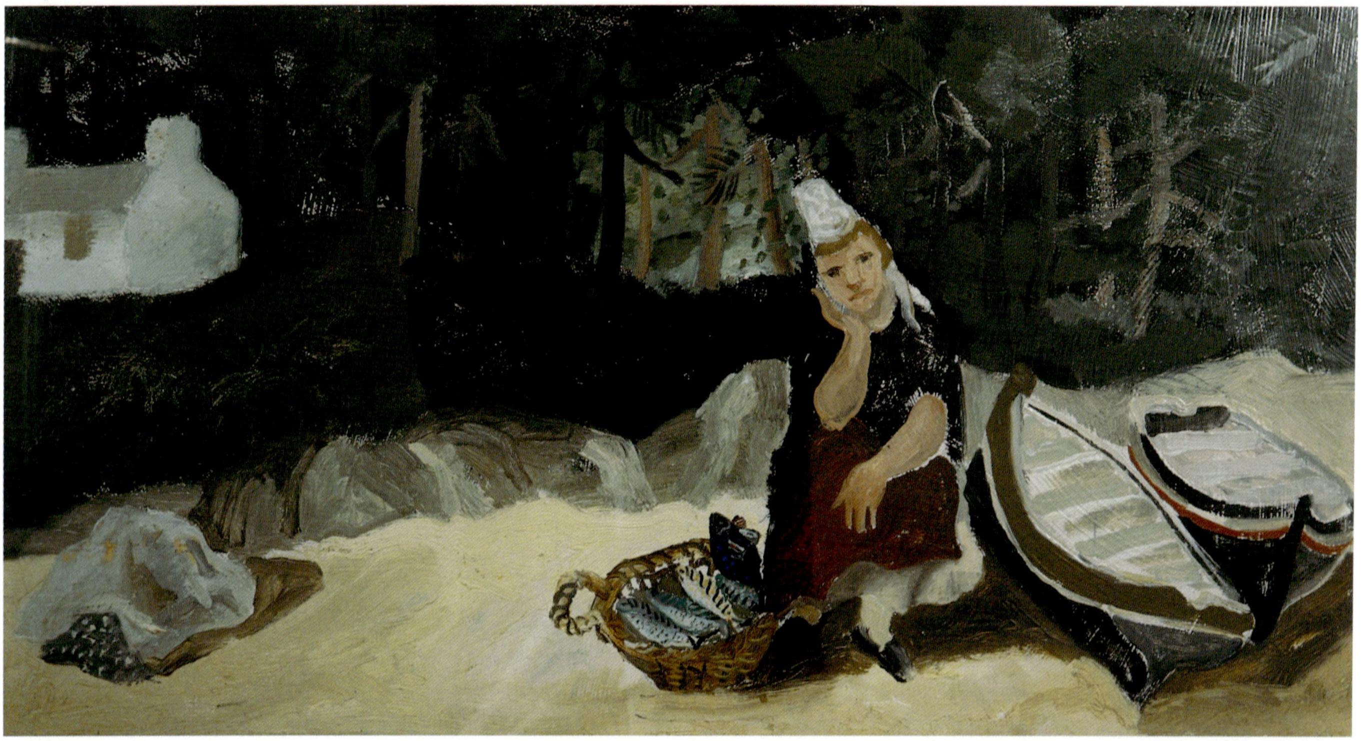

36 **Breton Fisherwoman** 1930

Oil on canvas 36.5 × 71.5 cm
The Dartington Hall Trust

Judging by her headdress, which is typical of the Quimper region, Wood painted this woman during one of his rare excursions outside Douarnenez. Unlike his St Ives paintings, in the Breton works the fisherwomen are inseparable from the sea and boats. Wood emphasises their patience, their waiting and their participation. They appear on clifftops, at shipyards, or darning nets. This woman, waiting patiently, anchored as solidly to the beach as the rocks, has been given masculine features. The basket and two boats also appear in *Sleeping Fisherman, Ploaré, Brittany* (no.26).

FS-C

37 **Building the Boat, Tréboul** 1930

Oil on board 58.4 × 83.3 cm
Kettle's Yard, University of Cambridge
[Exhibited in Quimper only]

Despite the title given to this work in Eric Newton's catalogue, this painting actually depicts a shipyard in la place de l'Enfer, Douarnenez, near the site of the Port Rhu.

Once again Wood based his composition on a photograph, while inserting other recurring elements. Thus the framework of the boat under construction can also be seen in another painting of the same period, *The New Boat, Tréboul* (no.38). In the background of both paintings can be seen the same cliff, on which stand little white and grey houses.

Always responsive to scenes of human activity and local trades, Wood has infused life into this composition, dominated by the boat's massive hull, by introducing a few figures. The two shipwrights, one seen from the back and the other in profile, and the melancholy looking old woman who holds a heavy plank of wood tightly to her chest, feature in Wood's preparatory drawing (whereabouts unknown; photograph in archive of Kettle's Yard, Cambridge); two other gossiping women are caught unawares by the painter's gaze.

SB

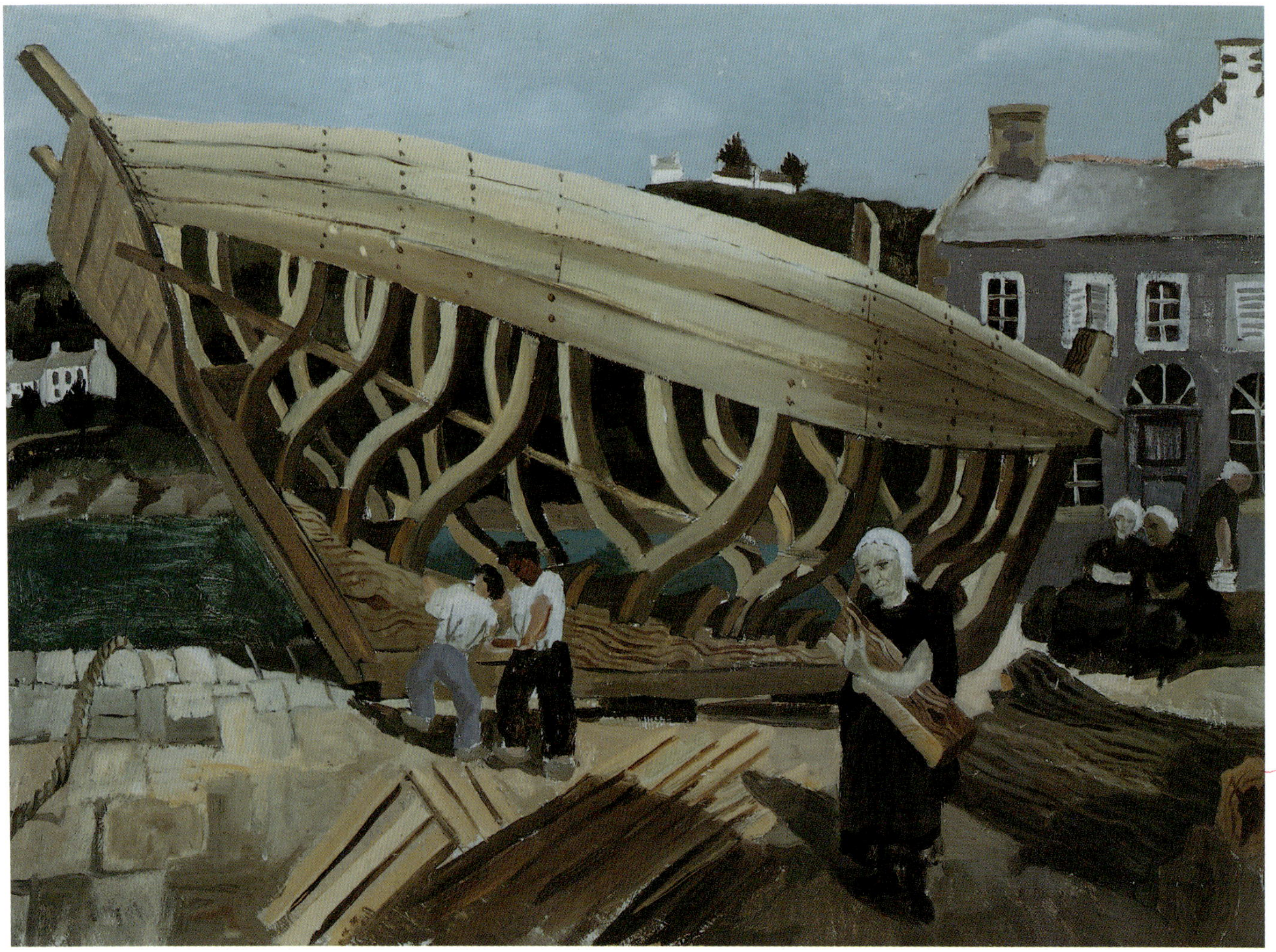

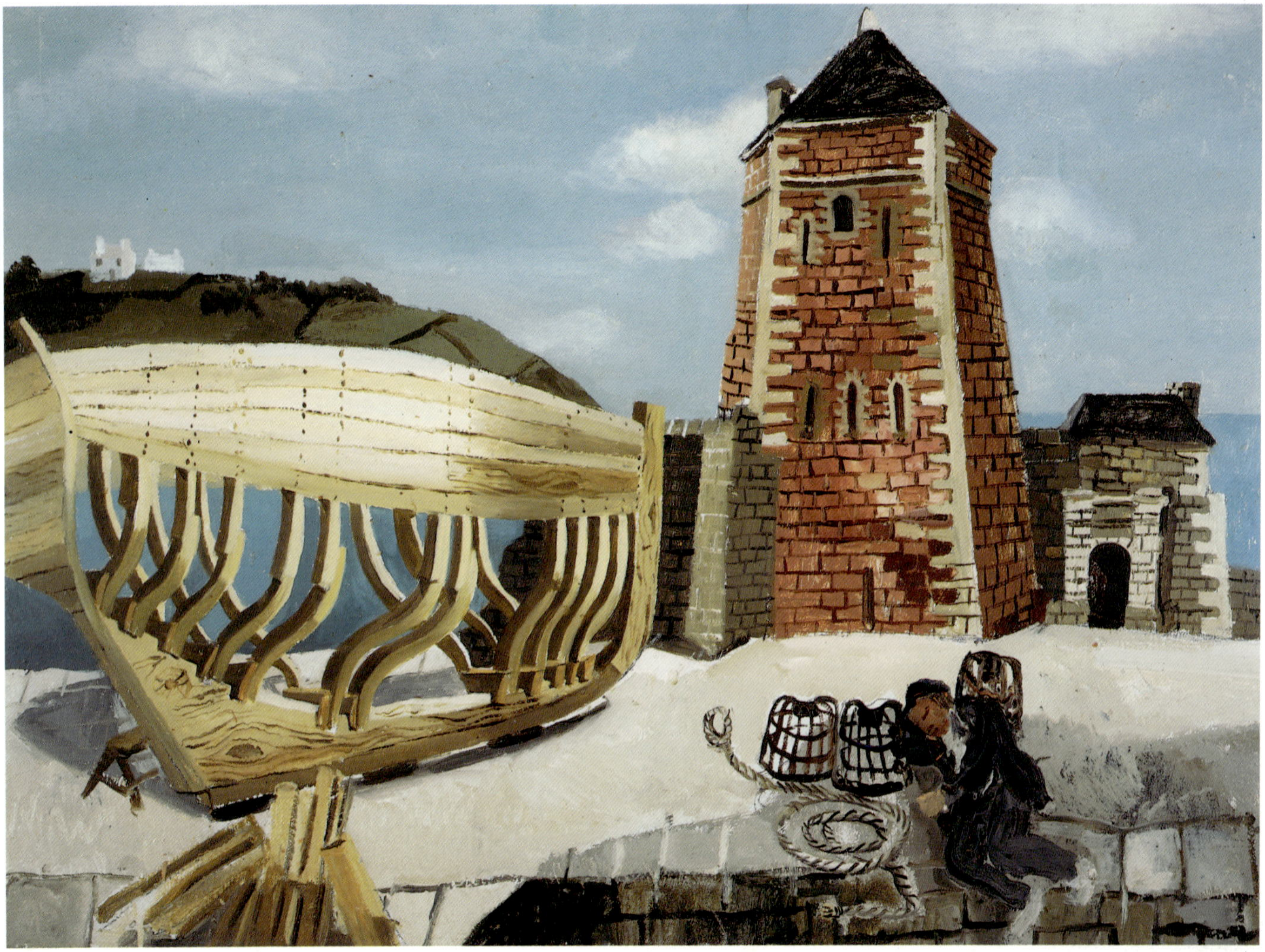

38 **The New Boat, Tréboul** 1930

Oil on canvas 56.5 × 81 cm
Private Collection
[Exhibited in St Ives only]

This work accurately depicts Fort Vauban at the entrance to Camaret harbour. Camaret-sur-mer is a small fishing port to the north-west of Tréboul and Douarnenez. There is no record of Wood having visited there, so we must speculate whether this image is based on a found photograph (fig.27 on p.24). The subject parallels *Building the Boat, Tréboul* (no.37). Although the architectural settings are different in the two works, the sleeping figure of the man here counters the woman carrying a plank in *Building the Boat*. In recalling Wood, Ede wrote of this imagery: 'He was very interested in the sadness of this scene … skeletons of ships in process of being built, which foreshadow the skeletons of the fishermen who would take them out and not return.' (H.S. Ede, *A Way of Life*, Cambridge 1984)

MT

39 **Boat in Harbour, Mousehole** 1930

Pen and ink wash 25.4 × 35.6 cm
Private Collection

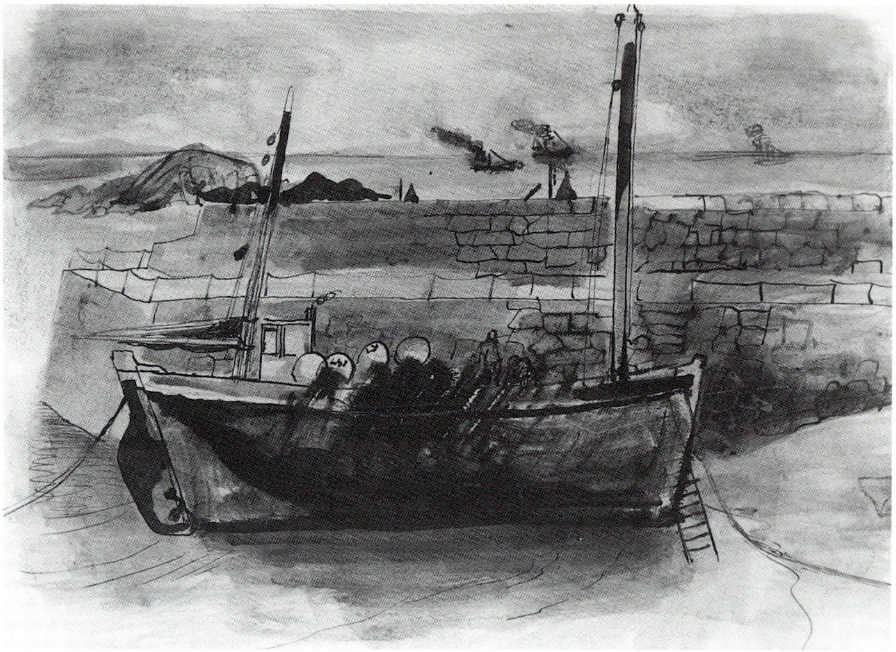

Wood produced a group of pen and ink drawings while in Mousehole, and although displaying certain similarities with finished paintings these remain far from provisional studies. Indeed Wood had abandoned this practice of drawing studies while in Cornwall two years earlier. As he wrote to Winifred Nicholson in 1928: 'I know all my boats and things without making drawings anymore' (TGA 8618). Wood appears to have been attracted back to the medium at this time, perhaps for its speed of working and sense of vitality which he was able to achieve in the drawn line.

In *Boat in Harbour, Mousehole* Wood expresses the feeling of the protection offered by the harbour, by accentuating the height of the wall beside the beached boat. The inclusion of half-glimpsed sails of other fishing boats over the wall and distant steamers on the rough seas adds to the sense of mystery and danger beyond the confines of the harbour.

MR

40 **Self-Portrait** c.1930

Pencil on paper 28 × 24 cm
Private Collection

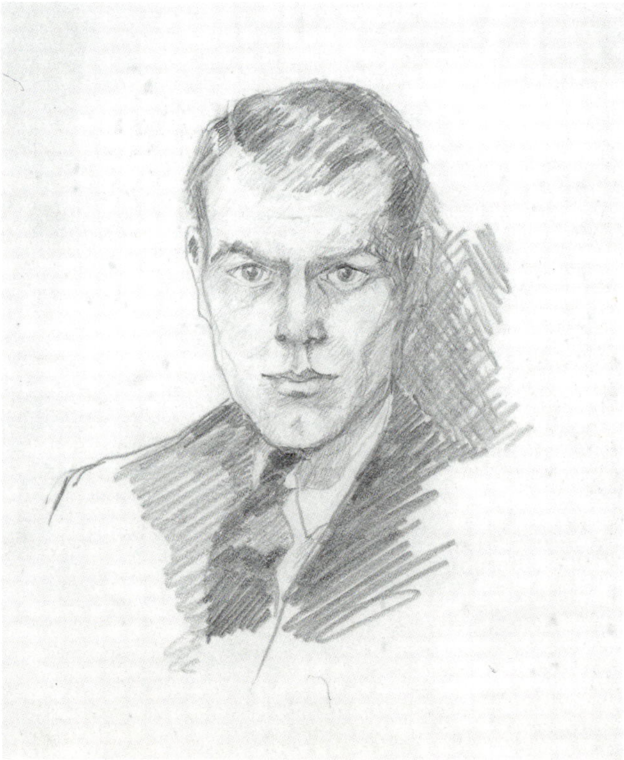

This drawing bears no date but has been tentatively ascribed to the last year of Wood's short life. The urgency of the drawn line, in particular the overdrawn contour of the face, and the gaunt features support this. It perhaps represents a late moment of self-reflection during a period of psychological and emotional instability for the artist brought on by his attempts to beat his opium addiction, before his tragic death at Salisbury station on 21 August 1930.

MR

Chronology

1901
7 April: Christopher Wood born in Knowsley, near Liverpool.

1907–15
Is educated at Freshfield Preparatory School and Marlborough.

1918
Studies medicine at Malvern College for one term.

1919
Studies architecture at Liverpool University.

1920
Leaves university and moves to London where he works as an apprenticed fruit importer.

1921
March: travels to Paris with banker Alphonse Kahn and moves into Kahn's house. Kahn arranges a studio for Wood at 54 rue des Saints Pères. Enrols at Académie Julian and later Grande Chaumière. Is introduced to Antonio de Gandarillas, honorary Chilean diplomat, who finances Wood's own flat.

1922
Travels through Europe to North Africa and Greece with Gandarillas. On his return to Paris he effectively moves in with Gandarillas.

1923
March: travels to south of France and Italy. Returns to Paris by the end of May. Is introduced to Picasso by Mme Errazuriz, Gandarillas's aunt.

1924
March: travels to Italy. August: travels to south of France, reaching Villefranche by late October where he meets Jean Cocteau for the first time. On his return to Paris he invites Cocteau to share his studio, an arrangement which lasts until February 1925.

1925
In Paris and London. Approaches Serge Diaghilev, who turns down his proposal to produce designs for a ballet called *English Country Life*.

1926
Diaghilev commissions designs from Wood for his forthcoming version of *Romeo and Juliet* but ultimately rejects them. August: travels to Cornwall with Gandarillas, visiting the Isles of Scilly and Penzance before reaching St Ives in early September. Stays on alone until October. On his return to London is introduced to Ben and Winifred Nicholson by Cedric Morris.

1927
Spends spring in Paris and London. February: paintings included in Seven and Five Society exhibition in London. August: travels to south of France.

1928
March and April: visits the Nicholsons at Banks Head, their home in Cumberland. Early summer: stays in Paris, where he meets Froska Munster – she becomes his mistress. August: is invited to join the Nicholsons at Feock, Cornwall, where he in turn is joined by Munster. Late August: goes with Ben Nicholson on a trip to St Ives, where they first encounter Alfred Wallis. Mid September – early December: stays in St Ives, initially with Munster and the Nicholsons, who also rent a house, but later alone.

1929
April: visits Dieppe with Munster. July: travels from Paris to Brittany. Early August – September: stays in Douarnenez and Tréboul. Meets the poet Max Jacob at Hôtel Ty-Mad.

1930
March: spends three weeks in Mousehole, Cornwall. June: attends opening of his exhibition in Paris, before travelling to Tréboul where he stays with Jacob at the Hôtel Ty-Mad until the end of July. 21 August: travels to Salisbury to meet his mother, where he is killed by a train at the railway station.

Further Reading

Andreu, Pierre, *Vie et mort de Max Jacob*, Paris 1982

Berlin, Sven, *Alfred Wallis: Primitive*, Bristol 1992

Clough, Paul, *Christopher Wood*, exh. cat., Kettle's Yard Gallery, Cambridge 1974

Collins, Judith, *A Painter's Place*, exh. cat., Abbot Hall Art Gallery, London 1991

Coquet, Françoise, 'Portraits des amis: Max Jacob et Christopher Wood en Bretagne', *Adam International Review*, no.487.492, 1988

Coquet, Françoise, 'Le Poète et le peintre, Jean Cocteau et Christopher Wood', *Franco British Studies*, no.12, Autumn 1991

Cross, Tom, *Painting the Warmth of the Sun: St Ives Artists* 1939–1945, Guildford 1984

Ede, H.S., *A Way of Life*, Kettle's Yard, Cambridge 1984

Faulks, Sebastian, *The Fatal Englishman: Three Short Lifes*, London 1996

Galerie de la Poste, *Max Jacob peintre*, exh. cat., Paris 1988

Gresty, Hilary, *Christopher Wood: The Last Years*, exh. cat., Newlyn Orion Gallery, Newlyn 1989

Harrison, Charles, *English Art and Modernism* 1900–1939, London 1981

Harrison, Charles, *The Modern, the Primitive and the Picturesque: Alfred Wallis, Chistopher Wood, Ben Nicholson*, exh. cat., Scottish Arts Council, Edinburgh, 1987

Hugo, Jean, *Le Regard de la mémoire*, Arles 1983

Ingleby, Richard, *Christopher Wood: An English Painter*, London 1995

Johnson, Penny and Judith Collins, *Adventure in Modern British Art under the Patronage of Lucy Wertheim*, exh. cat., Towner Art Gallery, Eastbourne 1992

Lewison, Jeremy, *Ben Nicholson*, exh. cat., Tate Gallery, London 1993

Lynton, Norbert, *Ben Nicholson*, London 1993

Mason, William, *Christopher Wood*, exh. cat., Arts Council of Great Britain 1979

Morphet, Richard, *Cedric Morris*, exh. cat., Tate Gallery, London 1984

Newton, Eric, *Christopher Wood*, Redfern Gallery, London 1938, 1959

Nicholson, Andrew (ed.), *Unknown Colour*, London 1987

Sachs, Maurice, *Au temps du Boeuf sur le Toit*, Paris 1987

Seckel, Hélène and André Cariou, *Max Jacob et Picasso*, exh. cat., Musée des Beaux-Arts, Quimper, Paris 1994

Wertheim, Lucy Carrington, *Adventures in Art*, London 1947

Whybrow, Marion, *St Ives*: 1883–1993: *Portrait of an Art Colony*, Woodbridge 1994

Willett, John, Sophie Bowness and Anna Gruetzner Robins, *The Dieppe Connection*, London 1992

Lenders

City of Aberdeen Art Gallery and Museums Collections 7, 8, 9

Bradford Art Galleries and Museums 15

Sir Michael Culme-Seymour Bt 6

The Dartington Hall Trust 17, 36

The Syndics of the Fitzwilliam Museum, Cambridge 23

Glasgow Museums: Art Gallery and Museum, Kelvingrove 30

Kettle's Yard, University of Cambridge 5, 14, 37

Laing Art Gallery, Newcastle upon Tyne (Tyne and Wear Museums) 26

Leeds Museums and Galleries (City Art Gallery) 22, 35

Leicestershire Museums Arts and Records Service 28

Lloyds TSB plc 24

Manchester City Art Galleries 4

Musée des Beaux-Arts, Quimper 13

Private Collection 2, 3, 18, 25, 27, 29, 31, 38, 39, 40

Sheffield City Art Galleries 10, 16, 21

Southampton City Art Gallery 20

Tate Gallery, London 11, 19, 32, 33

Towner Art Gallery and Museum, Eastbourne 1, 12, 34

Addenda

A conservation check is carried out on each work at the time of its arrival for the exhibition. On inspection, it was found that mediums for the catalogue entries listed below should read as follows:

no.5 Oil on canvas
no.8 Oil on board
no.17 Oil on board
no.18 Oil on board
no.26 Oil on board
no.28 Oil on board
no.30 Oil on board
no.36 Oil on board

Photographic Credits

In addition to the individuals and institutions listed above who kindly supplied photographs, the publishers would like to thank: Bob Berry; Bow Art; Bridgeman Art Library; A.C. Cooper Ltd; Anthony Hepworth Fine Art; Christopher Hurst; Richard Ingleby; Leach Studio; Kate Mount; Antonia Reeve Photography; Tate Gallery Photographic Department; John Webb

Index of Catalogued Works